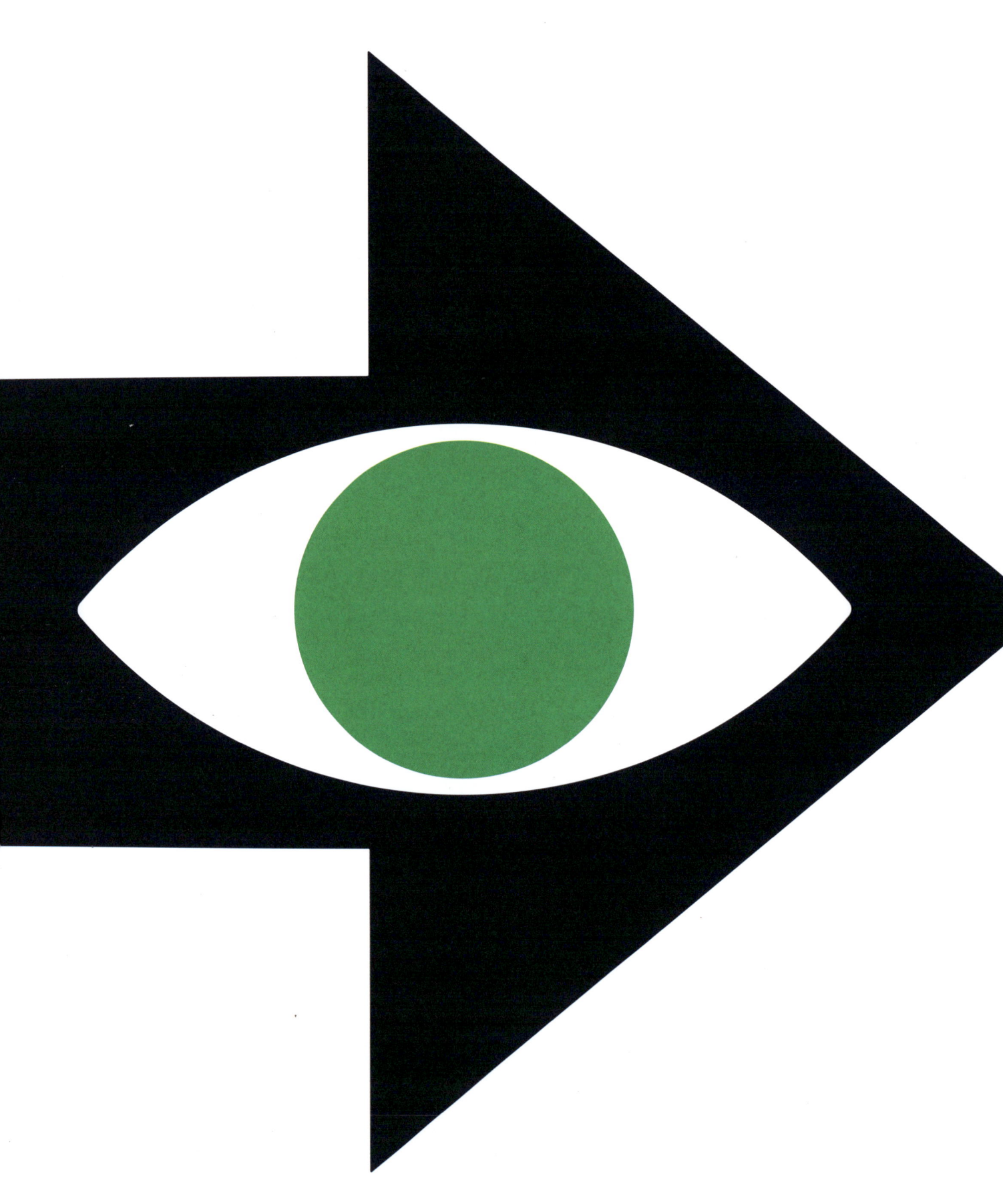

Eight Decades of British Design
Design Council 1944 to Today

Edited by Mark Cortes Favis

HALF TITLE PAGE Hans Schleger, logo for the Design Centre, 1955. Designed for the Design Centre in Haymarket, London, the public-facing showroom of the Design Council, then known as the Council of Industrial Design. It became a recognisable symbol of the organisation's founding commitment to promoting excellence in British industrial design

TITLE PAGE Design for Planet logo, 2023. Inspired by designer Bill Wallsgrove's suggestion, the Design Council's in-house team reinterpreted Schleger's 1955 logo to create the Design for Planet emblem, reflecting the Council's present-day mission to advance sustainable design in response to the climate emergency

Contents

6 **Editor's Note**
Mark Cortes Favis

8 **Partner's Foreword**
Liberty

10 **Introduction**
The Design Council at Eighty
Sir John Sorrell

16 **The 1940s**
Designing Industrial Recovery
Lesley Whitworth

30 **The 1950s**
Design and the Public
Lesley Whitworth and Penny Sparke

50 **The 1960s**
Design on the World Stage
Lesley Whitworth and Christopher Breward

70 **The 1970s**
Design in Flux
Lesley Whitworth and Jonathan M. Woodham

90 **The 1980s**
Design and Commerce
Lesley Whitworth and Deyan Sudjic

110 **The 1990s**
Design for a Connected World
Jeremy Myerson and Lynda Relph-Knight

130 **The 2000s**
Design for a New Millennium
Ellie Runcie and Max Fraser

150 **The 2010s**
Designing Through Uncertainty
Cat Drew and Mark Cortes Favis

170 **The 2020s**
Designing Our Future
Minnie Moll and Priya Khanchandani

192 Biographies
194 Picture Credits
195 About the University of Brighton Archives
Acknowledgements

Editor's Note
Mark Cortes Favis

Design is never static. It moves with us, shapes us and adapts to the forces that push and pull at society. It is a mirror of its time, responding to moments of crisis and celebration, to the quiet evolutions and sudden revolutions that transform the way we live, work and create. Over eight decades, British design has evolved in response to these shifts, and the Design Council has played a central role in that transformation. Its role has shifted from revitalising post-war industry to embedding design in business and public services, and, today, ensuring sustainability is at the heart of design practice across the UK.

As an American immersed in British design for two decades, including my time overseeing the publishing programme at the Design Museum as it made its historic relocation from Shad Thames to Kensington, I have witnessed how institutions evolve alongside the creative industries. This outsider's perspective has revealed the extraordinary ability of British design to absorb external influences while maintaining a distinct identity of its own.

This book unfolds across nine chapters, each exploring a different decade from the 1940s to today. Rather than presenting a purely object-based history of British design, it invites us to look through a wider lens – one able to frame the institutions, policies and cultural forces that have shaped the field. At its heart is the Design Council, which has both documented and influenced these changes through its evolving role in industry, education and public life.

Each chapter follows a structured approach: first examining the Design Council's activities, then exploring wider trends and movements, and finally featuring Liberty's perspective on print design and craftsmanship of that era. Throughout, the book weaves together expert analysis and first-hand perspectives from some of the most influential voices in the field.

Two key themes emerge through this eight-decade journey. The first is design as a reflection of change. Whether in moments of post-war rebuilding, industrial shifts, digital revolutions or sustainability movements, design has always been shaped by the currents of its time. As Lesley Whitworth details in the first chapter, the Design Council was founded in 1944 to revitalise

British industry after the war. In the decades that followed, design became a tool for commercial growth, social good, branding and storytelling, digital interaction and, most urgently today, addressing the climate crisis. Penny Sparke examines how public taste in design was shaped in the 1950s, while Max Fraser explores the 2000s as a turning point, as designers adapted to the digital era and globalisation.

The second theme is the expanding role of design. Once primarily concerned with well-made objects, design has evolved into a multidisciplinary force shaping everything from user experiences to government policies. Christopher Breward charts the 1960s as a period of radical change, as British design gained global recognition. Jonathan M. Woodham examines the professionalisation of design in the 1970s. By the 1980s, as Deyan Sudjic discusses, design became deeply intertwined with corporate identity. In the 1990s, as Lynda Relph-Knight explores, British design adapted to digitalisation and European integration. In the 2010s, as my own essay unravels, design was defined by disruption – challenging what design should be and who it serves.

This tension between leading and responding to change runs through British design's history. In some decades, designers have proactively shaped the future – in others, they have navigated economic and political pressures. Priya Khanchandani examines this in her exploration of the 2020s, our present moment, as design faces unprecedented challenges from climate crisis and artificial intelligence. What emerges clearly is that design continuously evolves, shifting in response to the world around it – sometimes pushing forward, sometimes being pulled along – from post-war reconstruction to today's fight against climate change.

I would like to thank the many contributors whose expertise has shaped this book, including those who have provided new research and insight into British design's evolving story. Thanks also to the Design Council, whose rich history provides the foundation for this project, and to Liberty, whose partnership has helped make this publication possible.

Looking ahead, may this book not only illuminate our design heritage, but also ignite fresh thinking about design's vital role in crafting tomorrow's world.

Partner's Foreword
Liberty

We are humbled and proud to work in partnership with the Design Council – the world's first publicly funded organisation dedicated to design. Liberty's innovative spirit, influential throughout the twentieth century, traces its unique DNA to the Arts and Crafts and the Aesthetic movements. Since our founding in 1875, Liberty has fostered a legacy of nurturing dialogue between art, design and nature. Now, as we carry forward this tradition by marking our 150th anniversary, we believe that design is about contributing to a sustainable world rooted in societal progress.

Andrea Petochi
Managing Director of Liberty
Chair of the British Museum Company

It was 150 years ago that Sir Arthur Lasenby Liberty – a British merchant with an adventurous and disruptive spirit – had the dream of docking a ship in the middle of London's streets. In 1875, that dream materialised when he chose Regent Street as the place to build what years later would become the flagship Liberty store, designed by Edwin T. Hall and his son Edwin S. Hall using the timbers of two historic ships. Liberty's collection of ornaments, fabric and objets d'art from around the world proved irresistible to Londoners, a social change in interior design and dress so significant that the Art Nouveau period in Italy was called the 'Liberty Style'. With such a rich history permeating the six floors of cutting-edge design, a visit to Liberty remains to this day a voyage of discovery.

Now used as a byword for the very best of textiles and design, Liberty is famed for its original curation, cultural collaborations and celebration of excellent craftsmanship. Located in the heart of London, the Liberty design studio is occupied by highly skilled artists who conceptualise, rework, colour and hand-draw hundreds of artworks, from archetypal, 1930s-style nostalgic florals and whimsical conversational pieces to bold geometrics, Indian-inspired chintzes,

ABOVE   Liberty store, Tudor building, 2024

BELOW Side view of the building's brick chimney stacks, 2021

dynamic abstractions and scenic landscapes. World-renowned for its historic 60,000-item design archive, Liberty has an in-house team of archivists who work tirelessly to collate the latest artworks while cataloguing the company's vast wealth of nineteenth- and twentieth-century designs. Former archivist Anna Buruma put it succinctly: 'If an archive isn't getting renewed, it slowly dies. It works both ways – we inspire the studio, and the studio gives back to us.'

Throughout its history, the Liberty design studio has worked with some of the finest couturiers. This began under the leadership of Liberty's Design Director of the late 1960s and early '70s, Bernard Nevill, who worked with icons such as Yves Saint Laurent and Cacharel using ingeniously reimagined prints drawn from the archive. Liberty continues to work with the equivalent of those brands today – testimony to the impact and timelessness of Liberty fabrics.

Central to this story is Liberty's signature Tana Lawn™ cotton from the 1920s. A masterpiece of fabric technology, Tana Lawn™ cotton is fine, cool and durable, with a soft and refined finish that captures the brilliance of Liberty's lustrous silks. Made from specially selected ultra-fine long staple fibres from Ethiopia, its bespoke manufacturing process has been fine-tuned by experts over the last 100 years. Advancing the product, Tana Lawn™ cotton now extends to Organic Tana Lawn™ and Tana Reborn, a fabric made from recycled Tana Lawn™ cotton. Introduced in 2025, Tana Reborn repurposes unused scraps of Tana Lawn™ cotton from Liberty's printing mill in Italy. These scraps are sorted, cleaned and shredded before being combined with virgin cotton to create a yarn containing recycled fibre.

Since 1875, Liberty has paved the way for a movement dedicated to discovery, animated by the arts, culture and design. In celebration of 150 years of Liberty, the company has partnered with the Design Council to weave together a history of British design from the 1940s to today. Each chapter in this book features an iconic Liberty print, showcasing the evolution of contemporary style across that decade. Encouraged by the Council's boundless creativity and commitment to making the world better through design, Liberty, as its creative partner, is proud to support and commemorate its eightieth anniversary.

RIGHT Liberty store, c.1920s

Introduction
The Design Council at Eighty
Sir John Sorrell CBE

Sir John Sorrell CBE is a designer, philanthropist and champion of the UK's creative industries. He was Chair of the Design Council (1994–2000) and a UK Business Ambassador, appointed by successive prime ministers to promote Britain's creative excellence. He chaired CABE (2004–09) and UAL (2013–18) and conceived the London Design Festival, chairing it from 2003 to 2023. He co-founded the London Design Biennale, serving as its president (2016–23). With Lady Frances Sorrell CBE, he ran Newell & Sorrell (1976–2000) and founded the Sorrell Foundation in 1999 to inspire young people's creativity. They later established the National Saturday Club, a free creative programme for 13–16-year-olds. A long-time advocate for design in education, business and culture, John reflects on his decades-long relationship with the Design Council in the following essay.

At eighty, I'm the same age as the Design Council. More than that, there are key aspects of my life in design that have intersected with some of the Council's most important milestones. I was born in London in February 1945, just weeks after the organisation first got up and running, and I have always felt a connection to the Design Council that runs deep.

Its creation was a visionary idea at a time of extreme danger for Britain, and it is a great example of creativity in the face of adversity. Towards the end of 1944, with World War II still far from over, Hugh Dalton, President of the Board of Trade in Winston Churchill's wartime government, was looking to Britain's future beyond the war. He set up what was initially called the Council of Industrial Design (CoID) in December 1944, with a mission to improve the design of British products, giving design a key role in Britain's economic recovery.

One of my earliest memories as a small child was being taken to the 1951 Festival of Britain. I was six years old. I remember the large crowds and the hum of excitement. The Council played a central role in the event, under the direction of Gordon Russell, who had been one of the Council's founding members. The Festival's big idea was to speed up the pace of change in the design of British-made goods. There was a collection of 10,000 industrial exhibits, and

ABOVE　　Portrait of Sir John Sorell, 2003
OPPOSITE　Exterior of The Design Centre, Haymarket, London, 1981. Frontage at night with illuminated neon signs above the entrance, representing Christmas presents with The Design Centre label

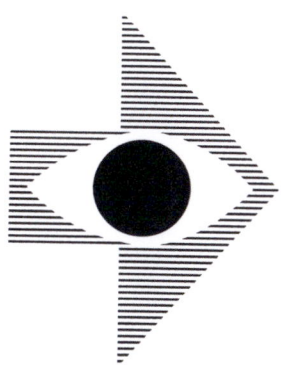

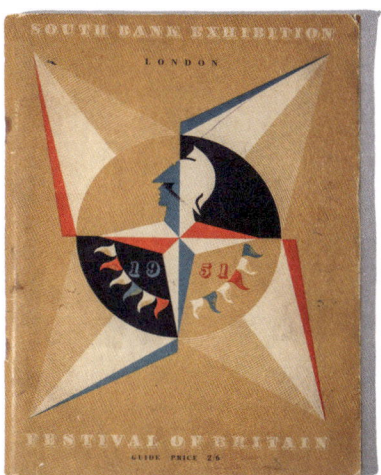

many of Britain's best designers and architects worked on the Festival, including Terence Conran, who was only twenty years old. Many years later, at the height of his success, he wrote,

> This highly successful exhibition which amazingly took place throughout the UK, although centred on London's South Bank, underscored Britain as the most creative nation in the world at a time it was smashed, grey and desolate. The great thing about the exhibition was that it demonstrated that there was a better life to be lived which could be achieved by intelligent creativity and pointed a way to a better quality of life. This made people happy, cheerful and positive, and even made a Spam sandwich taste good – well, not really – but it put a smile on people's faces. Some of them even cried with excitement, and it demonstrated that the UK had the ideas and know-how to create a modern world.

In the 1950s and '60s, as the Council campaigned vigorously for better use of industrial design and began to cultivate a high profile, I was learning about creativity and culture. I attended Saturday morning classes at Hornsey College of Art when I was fourteen, studied commercial art and design as a full-time student and qualified at nineteen to set up my first design business in 1964. I was aware of the Council's call for business and industry to take design more seriously and the Design Centre at their headquarters in Haymarket, with a programme of exhibitions, was an important backdrop as I made my first inexperienced steps trying to earn a living in design. I was also an avid reader of *Design* magazine, which was published by the Council, although I had little choice – there were very few alternatives at the time.

It was exciting to be a young designer in the '60s, a time of profound social and cultural change. Pop music and Pop art invigorated the design scene. Supersonic flight became a reality with the design icon Concorde. Neil Armstrong and Buzz Aldrin landed on the Moon. Anything seemed possible. It was good to see a series of intelligent initiatives by the Council, such as the Design Index and the

ABOVE Hans Schleger, symbol for The Design Centre for British Industries, 1955. Designed for the Council of Industrial Design, this logo appeared on Design Centre literature, publicity materials, displays and exhibitions (top); Cover of the *Festival of Britain Guide*, South Bank version, 1951 (bottom)

Design Advisory Service, and the expansion of its exhibition programme, as well as its name change to the more user-friendly Design Council. But nothing could halt the overall decline in British manufacturing, the coming of the slowdown and recession in the early '80s, and the 'Black Wednesday' financial crisis of 1992.

My wife Frances Sorrell (née Newell) and I set up our design company, Newell and Sorrell, in 1976 and by the beginning of the '90s we had developed a successful international business in corporate identity. With the Design Council focusing on engineering design, our paths diverged for a time. But in the early 1990s, we came back together unexpectedly. I was by now deeply involved in the design industry, on the board of the Chartered Society of Designers and chairman of the Design Business Association. Over lunch with a minister in 1991, I was asked if I would join the board for the Design Council, a role I gladly accepted.

However, I came upon a troubled organisation, widely viewed as out of touch with the shifting business, design and societal contexts of the time, and perilously close to being axed by the government. I was asked to attend a one-to-one meeting in Whitehall, at which it became clear that it would be a tough fight to keep the Council alive.

As described by Jeremy Myerson in the chapter of this book on the 1990s, I argued that the Design Council should not be shut down. It had been important to the nation in the past and could be so again. Nearly fifty years old at that time, its activities, narrative and the language around the organisation needed to change. It no longer required a director-general, for example, but a chief executive. It needed to promote a broader range of design disciplines and find out what its different audiences really required. Given support and some radical changes, I believed it could once again put Britain back in a design leadership role.

In September 1993, I was asked by Tim Sainsbury, the Minister for Industry, to lead a review. At this point, the Design Council's destiny and my own became entwined. The review was exhaustive – and exhausting. We consulted with hundreds of businesses, public bodies and educational institutions to develop a blueprint for a slimmer, sharper, more collaborative body with much more impact. In January 1994, my *Future Design Council* report landed on the minister's desk.

LEFT *Great Expectations,* 2001. Award-winning exhibition designed by Casson Mann for the Design Council as part of the UKinNY festival, displayed at Grand Central Station, New York

RIGHT *Creative Britain*, 31 March 1998. A Design Council report on behalf of Prime Minister Tony Blair

ABOVE Angus Hyland and Liz Farrelly, *Future Present: Millennium Products from the Design Council: It Just Takes One Good Idea*, editorial design by Pentagram, published by Booth-Clibborn Editions Ltd, 2000

Its recommendations were accepted in full, and I was then appointed Chairman of the Design Council.

Over the next six years, I was fortunate to have Frances and our colleagues take the weight of our business as I dedicated a large part of my life to the Council. First, we had to regain confidence, starting with the government. Several tactical initiatives would signal change and effectively reintroduce all echelons of the UK Government to the power of design. I wrote to all MPs and asked them to give me six minutes of their time, face to face, to hear why design and the Design Council were vital to the country. Many of them took up my offer and helped spread our message. To some people's surprise, we appointed a Design Director to the management team. We lobbied for Design Champions in every government department. There was no All-Party Parliamentary Group for design, so we started one with John Butcher and Mark Fisher as co-chairs. We found better, cheaper premises that were located more centrally in London – near the Houses of Parliament, so we could keep close to the government.

We celebrated the Council's fiftieth anniversary in 1995 with another initiative designed to catch people's imagination. Called Project 2045, it invited 2,045 people to design the future, asking, 'What will design be like in fifty years' time?' An exhibition at the Royal Festival Hall revealed some of their ideas, before they were all placed in time capsules and buried in locations around the UK, to be opened in the year 2045.

When Tony Blair came to power in 1997, the Design Council was right at the heart of Creative Britain and Cool Britannia, rebranding global perceptions of the country. In fact, Blair's first industry reception at 10 Downing Street, just after the election, was for designers.

After being out in the cold, the Design Council was now back at the centre of things. So much so that our Millennium Products initiative to identify 1,000 outstanding examples of British design and innovation was officially launched by Blair at BBC Television Centre in September 1997, and unveiled in December 1999 on the site of the Millennium Dome.

As we entered the twenty-first century, the *Millennium Products* exhibition toured the world, promoting British creativity with a series of installations in unusual venues, such as Grand Central Station in New York. In 1998, our *Creative Britain* report, on behalf of the prime minister, set out the progress of the Design Council's work and looked to the future.

I stepped down as chairman in 2000 and went on to new challenges and initiatives, such as the creation of the London Design Festival and the London Design Biennale, and to focus on the educational foundations Frances and I created – the Sorrell Foundation in 1999 and the National Saturday Club in 2009. My work now centres on education, especially on the 2,000 members of the National Saturday Club.

Recently, I returned to an issue that has preoccupied the Design Council at different times in its history: namely, defining what design is. When I was first appointed chairman of the Council, I had to give a lot of speeches followed by questions from the audience. 'What is design?' always came up. I became tired of explaining that there are many definitions, and so decided to produce a little book titled *Definitions of Design*. It had fifty contributors and was published in 1995 by the Design Council to celebrate its fiftieth anniversary.

A couple of years ago, I decided to recycle my idea. I invited 100 people to contribute to a new book that is titled *What is Design? 100 Definitions*. Here are just two of my favourites, one from the original book thirty years ago and one from the new edition:

With art – if you like – you can be really weird. But in design you have to think about what other people will like.
— Ghisli, aged 10

Design is intuition in the service of utility, economy and grace.
— Nicholas Serota

I have also taken great interest in the continuing journey of the Design Council. Like all eighty-year-olds, it has had its ups and downs. It has battled through periods of adversity. But it has had many periods of great success, when it has been brilliant at helping create a brighter future for Britain. Today, the Design Council is flying the sustainability flag amid a global climate emergency and its success is vitally important. I wish it well.

The 1940s

Designing Industrial Recovery

Foundations for a New Britain: Origins of the Design Council
Lesley Whitworth

What is a council, and how can the story of *the* Council – the Design Council – be told? Who should appear? The politicians and activists whose combined efforts created it, the revolving members of its eminent policymaking inner circle, the staff who made it work, the diverse bodies with which it cooperated? A cast of thousands could be added for this particular organisation: manufacturers, designers, commentators, educators, retailers, co-sponsors, fellow travellers, competition winners, and the British and other buying publics. More complex than an individual biography and open to multiple interpretations, a council – especially one as long-lived as the Design Council – is a different entity at different times. Contexts create change: the party in government, the economy, research. The celebratory account that begins here signposts this texture.

The decision to establish what was originally called the Council of Industrial Design, with its Scottish Committee, was announced to Parliament on 19 December 1944 by Hugh Dalton, President of the Board of Trade. A preliminary meeting happened on 28 December, and in May 1945 a staff of ten moved to Tilbury House, Petty France, London, where its executive began work. From the autumn, its concerns were redirected to the *Britain Can Make It* exhibition planned for 1946 by a new Board of Trade president, Sir Stafford Cripps, keen to rally the country behind a bold industrial vision.

Design and innovation now being such ubiquitous ideas, it's difficult to imagine a time before such professional activity was recognised. Hard, too, to grasp that rationing and controls still governed the quantity and quality of essential goods up to the early 1950s.[1] How was it possible that state sponsorship of design-promotion seemed necessary and urgent, even before World War II ended in 1945?

The idea had both a two-century gestation and an immediate provenance. The longer story embraces the Royal Society for the Encouragement of Arts, Manufactures and Commerce (RSA), the Great Exhibition, the Royal College of Art, the British Institute of Industrial Art and the Council for Art and Industry, among much else.[2] The urgent prompt involved peacetime readaptation and a

ABOVE Early meeting of the policy-making body of the Council of Industrial Design, 1945
PREVIOUS PAGE View along the Thames river, showing smoke rising from the London docks following an air raid during the Blitz, 1940

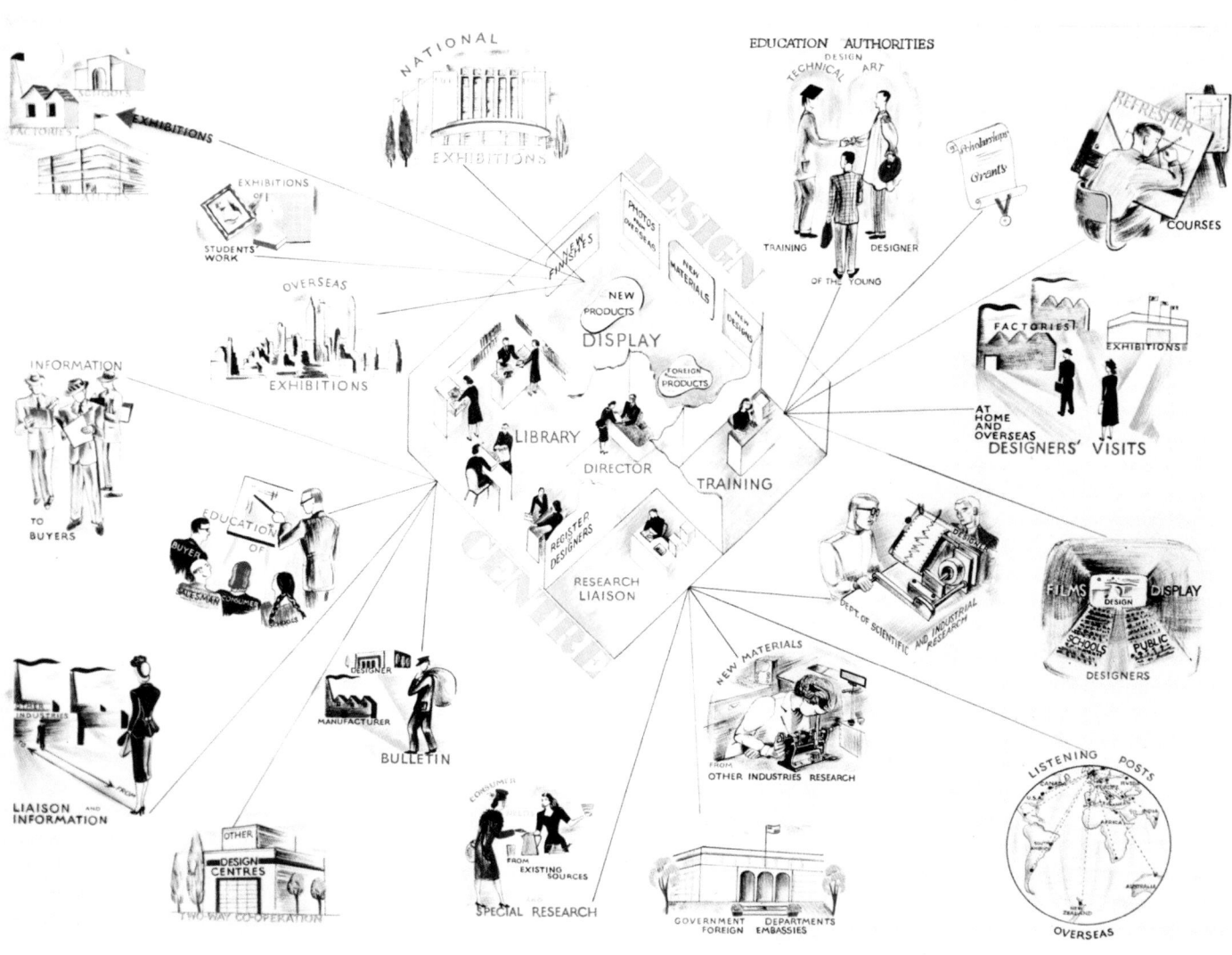

ABOVE Illustration of the proposed working of a design centre, drawn by Miss Disher, c.1947

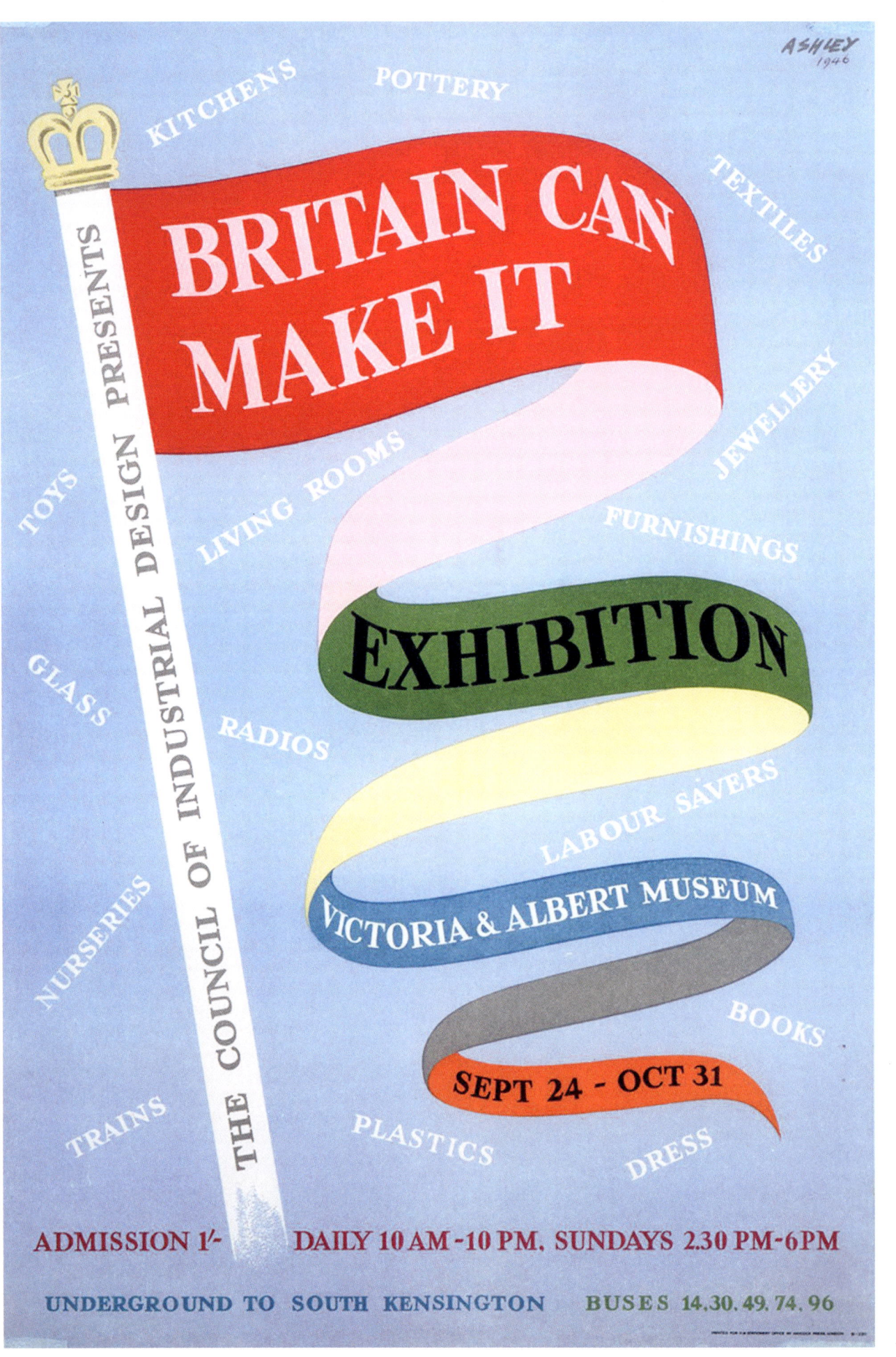

OPPOSITE Ashley Havinden, *Britain Can Make It* poster, 1946. A pioneering British graphic designer and art director, Havinden was known for his modernist typography and bold advertising work, which helped define mid-century commercial design

BELOW Queues on Exhibition Road outside the V&A, waiting to visit *Britain Can Make It*, 1946

looming balance-of-payments crisis should the UK's war-ravaged manufacturing sector not prove equal to its competitors'.³

To avoid creating too unwieldy a 'representative' body, Council members were chosen for the breadth of their individual interests and their known commitment to design. Launching their mission, Dalton urged:

> If you succeed in your task, in a few years' time every side of our daily life will be the better for your work. Every kitchen will be an easier place to work in; every home a pleasanter place to live in. Men and women in millions will be in your debt, though they may not know it.⁴

It was to be 'a teamwork of partners' and a process of engagement and persuasion.⁵ Beyond industry, it 'appeared essential' to reach schools, the distributive trades and all 'those voluntary organisations which seemed best able to take effective interest in the subject of design'.⁶ In practice, this first period was spent making overtures to voluntary and official bodies with kindred concerns, systematising the Council's dialogue with industry and acting 'in co-operation with interested State departments', providing advice when asked.⁷

The Council did not seek to usher in the 'mammoth runs characteristic of certain American industries' or impose an orthodoxy.⁸ Nevertheless, a misconception lingered that the Council supplied approved designs.⁹ What it *could* do, following its assumption of responsibility for a list of industrial designers formerly operating at the behest of the Board of Trade, was to make introductions for manufacturers. Reckoning it to be 'the most complete list in existence', this Record of Designers stood at 626 names in 1948, rising to 1,000 the following year.¹⁰ A decade later, the Council reckoned this to be 'one of the most valuable contributions that [it] makes to British industry'.¹¹

Fuelled by exhibition planning, staff numbers accelerated past a hundred by spring 1946, although they dropped back afterwards. The *Britain Can Make It* exhibition represented a social and economic manifesto founded on design, making immense demands on the youthful organisation. The full-time effort of

RIGHT James Gardner working on a maquette for the exhibition, and a finished stand in 'Shop Window Street' at *Britain Can Make It*, 1946. A leading British museum and exhibition designer, Gardner was known for his dynamic, visitor-focused approach, shaping some of the most significant exhibitions of the mid-twentieth century

OVERLEAF Detail from the 'War to Peace' section of the exhibition, relating aluminium saucepans to a damaged aircraft fuselage, 1946

each industrial liaison officer was needed to locate sufficient products of merit to display in the space made available in the Victoria and Albert Museum.[12] Final visitor numbers of nearly 1.5 million were sixty per cent higher than expected.[13] Public demand for admission tested, and indeed overstrained, the capacity of the museum for many weeks. The exhibition was extended for a month, and then another month. At least 43,000 British trade visitors attended, plus 7,000 from overseas. Unofficial press estimates of the volume of orders placed ranged from £25 million to £50 million. There were 1,297 firms with products included, 2,300 journalists came and ten separate films were made about it.

It being impossible to translate the exhibition wholesale to Scotland, an equivalent offering opened in the Royal Scottish Museum, Edinburgh, in late August 1947. Nearly half a million people attended *Enterprise Scotland*, and from January 1948 its counterpart, *Enterprise Travels*, found appreciative audiences in Hamilton, Ayr, Dumfries, Galashiels, Stirling, Cupar, Dundee and Perth.[14] The following year, an estimated 120,000 visited the Scottish Committee's 'New Furniture' display at Kelvin Hall, Glasgow, where an associated event for industrial workers and apprentices was oversubscribed and had to be repeated over several evenings.[15]

A London exhibition space created at Murray House, next to Tilbury House, in 1947 was initially underused, as Council activities happened elsewhere. It began its long associations with the British Industries Fair, the Building Exhibition and the *Daily Mail* Ideal Home Exhibition, at which 140,000 saw its displays.[16] Two years later, when it furnished three flats and a house built by the Ministry of Health at the same show, numbers doubled to 280,000.[17] A regional circuit of Design Weeks and Design Fairs, featuring Council and retail displays, talks and forums, with the support of Chambers of Commerce, civic dignitaries, libraries, art galleries and museums, brought communities distant from London into the debate.

The overseas work of the Exhibition Division attracted significant praise for what was clearly an experimental foray into collaboration with the British Council, staging the national component of a small, international exhibition of

ABOVE 'Design Fair' display by Alec Heath, Manchester City Art Gallery, 1948

LEFT 'Design Week' window display, Lewis's Ltd, Birmingham, 1948

RIGHT *This or That?*, a publication for young readers written by Wyndham Goodden and illustrated by Barbara Jones, published by the Council's Scottish Committee, 1947
BELOW Staff in the library at Tilbury House, 1947

industrial design held by the Bond voor Kunst in Industrie at the Stedelijk Museum Amsterdam in April 1949. A leading Dutch journalist wrote that, 'The English [sic.] section rises head and shoulders above the others… These objects speak of a modern civilisation.' It was widely considered to have stolen the show.[18]

Beyond exhibition attendance, the appetite for information about new equipment, new materials and new ideas cannot be underestimated. A poster about the 'Things We Use' prepared by the Bureau of Current Affairs with Council cooperation sold a thousand copies.[19] *Design '46*, which accompanied *Britain Can Make It*, sold over 60,000 copies there and about 45,000 through the trade at a premium price of six shillings.[20] Demand for talks so far exceeded the Council's capacity to provide them that, from July 1948, it maintained a list of capable speakers eventually running to nearly 300 names.[21] There were 237 presentations coordinated during the reporting year 1949–50.[22] Less-accomplished speakers were supported with lecture notes or recorded commentaries. The Council's first film strip was called *Our Homes* and covered 'the social background of design'.[23]

All sets of its 'boxed exhibitions' were in constant use from September 1947, and the loan process was ultimately streamlined because of demand, with sets permanently relocated to libraries, museums and art galleries.[24]

Consistent contributions to trade journals, daily newspapers and popular magazines showed the Council's determination, the energy of its emergent publishing arm and the potential audience for such material. A weekly bulletin of design-related content gleaned from British and foreign technical journals was developed for internal use, but from 1947 'Design Abstracts' of eight to ten pages and sixty to seventy items gained 200 subscribers.[25] A 'Design Calendar' listing exhibitions and lectures in London and the regions was circulated free to 4,000 recipients in education and industry.[26] By March 1949, over 1,400 schools were subscribing to the Design Folio series at fifty shillings per set.[27] A 'substantial postal service' of book loans, periodicals and requested information was also sustained.[28]

LEFT   The Council working with the BBC on the set of *Making a Chair*, showing Frank Austin, 1947

BELOW   Cover of the Council's professional journal *Design*, launched in 1949

Council publications were initially printed by His Majesty's Stationery Office, with a usual price range of sixpence up to one shilling and sixpence.[29] Over £2,000-worth of Design Fair guides and other inexpensive booklets were sold at this and similar events during the year.[30] The cost of teaching aids typically ranged from two shillings and three pence up to five shillings; others were loaned.[31] Out of receipts totalling £20,051 in 1948–9, more than £15,000 was generated through sales of publications, representing some 254,000 items.[32]

Three Council films were made with varying degrees of success. All copies of the first were ordered to be destroyed, so unhappy were they with the results. The second, *Designing Women* (1947), starring Joan Greenwood and Joyce Grenfell, was sold to Piccadilly Films Ltd. The Scottish Committee worked with Pathé, and *A Question of Taste* gave self-presentation advice to young women, narrated by Hardy Amies. The Council's publicity team also joined forces with the BBC to share the 'good design' message in some early television programming.[33]

Having barely had time to establish its normal operations, the Council's energies were diverted again following Herbert Morrison's December 1947 announcement of government support for a Festival of Britain in 1951, marking the centenary of the Great Exhibition. The number of industrial-liaison officers immediately leapt from three to eighteen, as the need to survey and galvanise manufacturers became critical.[34] In 1948, staff began systematically collating product details on a 'pictorial card index' to support planning, and by the following spring it had 1,400 entries.[35] This Stock List was later repurposed for display on the South Bank as a Design Review, as it supplemented 'the comparatively limited number of actual manufactured exhibits' for which there was space.[36]

In January 1949, the Council took the logical step of launching a periodical called *Design*. By December, it was already attracting readers beyond those intended, including in art and technical schools.[37] In the period to January 1953, its masthead went from 'a monthly journal for manufacturers and designers' to 'the journal for manufacturers and designers', then 'the magazine for

manufacturers, designers and retailers' before, finally, confidently abandoning a masthead.

Late in the decade, the Council could reflect with satisfaction that visitors from 'almost every country' had called at its offices during the year.[38] Its settled activities included Design Advice, Design Review, the Record of Designers and, from 1949, *Design*. The centrality of retail to its mission had become clear, constituting nodes in a communication matrix, especially with the public.[39] A meeting with retailers from the Midlands in early 1949 confirmed that staff training might be the most productive contact between the Council and this sector. Great hope was also invested in pragmatic engagement with children of school age, as part of a larger aim 'to stimulate a critical public demand for good design'.[40]

Any fair-minded review of this first half-decade of Council activity must conclude that – despite the immense newness of the venture, the paucity of resources and the audacity of its vision – a resounding start was made. The building blocks of virtually every activity that would characterise its future programme were in place, and the Council could congratulate itself that its press office had 'secured a considerable volume of publicity' for its agenda and that it had 'pursued energetically its policy of persuasion and education on as broad a front as possible within the limits of its time and funds'.[41]

1. See Ina Zweiniger-Bargielowska, *Austerity in Britain: Rationing, Controls and Consumption, 1939–1955* (Oxford: OUP, 2000); and Judy Attfield (ed.), *Utility Reassessed: The Role of Ethics in the Practice of Design* (Manchester: MUP, 1999).
2. The Council's first *Annual Report* included a two-page appendix listing significant precursors and influential reports. For a fuller sense of this backstory, see Antony J. Coulson, *A Bibliography of Design in Britain, 1851–1970* (London: Design Council, 1979). See also Louise Purbrick (ed.) *The Great Exhibition of 1851: New Interdisciplinary Essays* (Manchester: Manchester University Press, 2001) and Yasuko Suga, '"Purgatory of Taste" or Projector of Industrial Britain? The British Institute of Industrial Art', *Journal of Design History*, 16/2 (2003), 167–85.
3. See Paddy Maguire, 'Designs on Reconstruction: British Business, Market Structures and the Role of Design in Post-War Recovery', *Journal of Design History*, 4/1 (1991), 15–30.
4. Cited in CoID, *Annual Report, 1945–46*, 6. On the Council's sense of mission, see Jonathan M. Woodham, 'Design and the State: Post-War Horizons and Pre-Millenial Aspirations', in D. J. Huppatz (ed.), *Design: Critical and Primary Sources*, Volume 4: *Development, Globalization, Sustainability* (London and New York: Bloomsbury, 2016), 99–114, and Lesley Whitworth, 'Collective Responsibility: The Public and the (UK) Council of Industrial Design in the 1940s', in Harriet Edquist and Laurene Vaughan (eds.), *The Design Collective: An Approach to Practice* (Newcastle upon Tyne: Cambridge Scholars, 2012), 164–81.
5. CoID, *Annual Report, 1945–46*, 12.
6. CoID, *Annual Report, 1948–49*, 17.
7. CoID, *Annual Report, 1945–46*, 18 and 22. It also furnished show homes, gave evidence to industry working parties and assisted the British Intelligence Objectives Sub-Commitee. On the latter, see Nikolaus Pevsner et al. in Anne Sudrow (ed.), *Geheimreport Deutsches Design: Deutsche Konsumgüter im Visier des Britischen Council of Industrial Design* (1946) (Wallstein, 2012) (contains material in English).
8. CoID, *Annual Report, 1945–46*, 23.
9. CoID, *Annual Report, 1948–49*, 14.
10. CoID, *Annual Report, 1947–48*, 6, and CoID, *Annual Report, 1948–49*, 15.
11. CoID, *Annual Report, 1958–59*, 8.
12. See Diane Bilbey (ed.), *Britain Can Make It: The 1946 Exhibition of Modern Design* (London: Paul Holberton in association with V&A Publishing, 2019); Patrick J Maguire and Jonathan M. Woodham (ed.); *Design and Cultural Politics in Postwar Britain: The Britain Can Make It Exhibition of 1946* (London and Washington, DC: University of Leicester Press, 1997); Penny Sparke (ed.), *Did Britain Make It? British Design in Context, 1946–86* (London: Design Council, 1986).
13. All data cited in this paragraph: CoID, *Annual Report, 1946–47*, 4–5.
14. CoID, *Annual Report, 1947–48*, 16.
15. CoID, *Annual Report, 1948–49*, 27.
16. CoID, *Annual Report, 1947–48*, 12.
17. CoID, *Annual Report, 1948–49*, 4.
18. CoID, *Annual Review, 1949–50*, 6.
19. CoID, *Annual Report, 1946–47*, 15.
20. ibid., *Annual Report, 1946–47*, 14.
21. CoID, *Annual Report, 1948–49*, 19.
22. CoID, *Annual Report, 1949–50*, 24.
23. CoID, *Annual Report, 1946–47*, 15.
24. CoID, *Annual Report, 1947–48*, 9, and CoID, *Annual Report, 1949–50*, 26.
25. CoID, *Annual Report, 1947–48*, 11.
26. Ibid.
27. CoID, *Annual Report, 1948–49*, 19.
28. CoID, *Annual Report, 1946–47*, 16.
29. CoID, *Annual Report, 1947–48*, 8.
30. CoID, *Annual Report, 1948–49*, 18.
31. CoID, *Annual Report, 1947–48*, 9.
32. CoID, *Annual Report, 1948–49*, 21.
33. Michelle Jones, 'Design and the Domestic Persuader: Television and the British Broadcasting Corporation's Promotion of Post-war "Good Design"', *Journal of Design History*, 16/4 (2003), 307–18.
34. CoID, *Annual Report, 1948–49*, 9.
35. ibid., 12.
36. CoID, *Annual Report, 1949–50*, 5.
37. CoID, *Annual Report, 1948–49*, 20.
38. ibid., *1948–49*, 16.
39. CoID, *Annual Report, 1949–50*, 3.
40. ibid., 19. See also Jane Pavitt (ed.), *Object Lesson: The Camberwell Collection* (London: Camberwell College of Arts, 1996).
41. CoID, *Annual Report, 1947–48*, 10, and CoID, *Annual Report, 1949–50*, 2. YO

LIBERTY.

OPPOSITE Honeydew, 1930s

Honeydew
A Floral Legacy Reimagined

Reimagined in the Liberty design studio for Spring/Summer 2020, Honeydew was originally created in the 1930s. This delightful artwork is an ode to Liberty's iconic botanicals, featuring a graceful array of hand-painted dahlias, poppies, anemones, daisies and bluebells. Each floral element is finely illustrated with delicate outlines, encapsulating a traditional British cottage garden.

Romantic, dreamy and effortlessly chic, Liberty's heritage florals were informed by the spirit of the 1930s and '40s. This period of floral nostalgia was characterised by small, charming botanical motifs, which subsequently became emblematic of Liberty's distinctive style. Forever cherished and immortalised through print, these designs showcase exquisitely intricate gardens, windswept meadows and charming hedgerows. Typically featuring intricate outlines and printed with woodblocks, they were often coloured in soft pastel shades or used light, refreshing palettes. Liberty's quintessential style continues to be reinvented through contemporary techniques that bring renewed vigour and creative ingenuity.

The 1950s

Design and the Public

Design for a Better Britain: The Design Council Taking Root
Lesley Whitworth

Although perennially linked to the Festival of Britain,[1] the Council had just a single discrete responsibility: gathering industrially made exhibits.[2] Nevertheless, 1951 marked the culmination of three years' effort for this fledgling body, once more nudged from its core agenda. In practice, staff of its Industrial Division wrote text, too, for the South Bank, the Glasgow exhibition, a land-based touring exhibition and HMS *Campania*, the Festival ship. The Council also orchestrated the less well-known Design Congress, 'Design Policy in Industry as a Responsibility of High-Level Management', held in association with the Federation of British Industries; the Trades Union Congress; Royal Society for the Encouragement of Arts, Manufactures and Commerce; Royal College of Art; Society of Industrial Artists;[3] and the Design and Industries Association. Attendees came from fifteen countries and speakers from Sweden, the USA, Denmark, Holland and Italy.[4] By some estimates, almost half the population engaged with some aspect of this five-month celebration of national contributions in the fields of science, culture and arts, from a broad spectrum of popular and industrial arts. Within two months of the Festival's conclusion, some 3,500 loaned products were methodically returned by Council staff, a portent of the highly efficient exhibition team to come. Industrial officer numbers promptly reverted to four.[5]

Having proved 'unexpectedly popular' with visitors and deemed necessary to preserving manufacturers' interest, Design Review was destined for retention when the Korean War influenced a challenging twenty-five per cent loss of government grant-in-aid.[6] Its focus on durable consumer goods was narrowed – a constraint only fully reversed many years later. Such funding lurches became characteristic of the Council's existence.

Between May and December 1950, retailers chosen by lottery showed a touring version of the Council's furnished exhibit from the *Daily Mail* Ideal Home show (bottom of page 35). The selection process became necessary when the offer in the furniture trade press was hopelessly oversubscribed, despite a hiring fee for transportation, construction and maintenance costs.[7] There were show homes in the regions, although 'necessary economies' brought the successful series of Design Fairs to a halt after Hull in February 1950.[8]

ABOVE Gordon Russell showing Walter Gropius around the Design Centre shortly before its opening in April 1956. Photograph by Sam Lambert

PREVIOUS PAGE Festival of Britain, South Bank, London, 1951. View of the upstream section of the exhibition site, seen from the Waterloo Station entrance, with the Dome of Discovery and the Skylon in the distance

ABOVE 'Look Before You Shop', poster, Design Centre, 1956

LEFT — Display of seating at the Council of Industrial Design and the Corporation of Birmingham Manufacturers' Competition for the *Exhibition of Outdoor Seats*, 1953

BELOW — Pamphlet accompanying an *Exhibition of Outdoor Seats* submitted to the Council by manufacturers, 1953. Embankment Gardens, courtesy of London County Council

RIGHT — Interior of the Design Centre in Haymarket, London, showing the main display space (left); Interior of the Scottish Design Centre in Glasgow, 1959 (right)

BELOW The interests of audiophiles were met by the Design Centre exhibition *Hi-Fi*, poster, 1959

The Ministry of Transport's request that the Council engage with street furniture quickly bore fruit.[9] *Design* magazine was being imaginatively utilised: GEC (General Electric Company) bought a thousand copies of March 1952's issue for its agents worldwide, reporting that it was 'well worthwhile'; the Rayon Industry Design Centre bought and distributed 1,500 copies each month in 1952.[10] Foreign circulation was also increasing. In one month (March 1954), new subscriptions came in from eighteen different countries.[11] Equally, the first edition of *Design and Our Homes*, published jointly with the Co-Operative Union for a popular readership, sold out and was reprinted immediately.[12] Interest in design burgeoned.

Conceptually, the Council's new headquarters at Haymarket, London, was a 'joint venture of government and industry'; practically, it benefited from significant input from the Board of Trade and the Ministry of Works; realistically, it required a show of faith in the form of substantial donations from a broad spectrum of companies and individuals committed to its aims (pages 32–33).[13] Government willingness to bear most of the setting-up costs for this 'Design Centre for British Industries' was predicated on recognition of its national importance as a permanent showcase for design excellence. As a precursor, sufficient goods suitable for display needed to be in production, and manufacturers needed to be won round to the principle of selective exhibition. To this end, three additional field officers intensified the work of outreach and liaison in the run-up to the opening. Engagement with a providentially rich national tapestry of trade associations, just as preceded 1946 and 1951, contributed to a surge of a thousand visits.

HRH Prince Philip, Duke of Edinburgh, opened the Design Centre on 26 April 1956, expressing the hope that it would provoke controversy. It now became the great engine of Council activity, and retailers helped magnify its impact: 118 shops up and down the country created displays sympathetic to its opening and others hung posters. Talks were arranged in places as diverse as Dartford and Cambridge.[14] Consciousness of different family scenarios informed the Centre's displays, meeting various price points and budgets: it was intended for 'a very wide public'.[15]

RIGHT Leaflets for show homes furnished by the Council in association with (left) *Manchester Evening News* and Sale Borough Council and (right) *Birmingham Mail* and Corporation of Birmingham, 1951

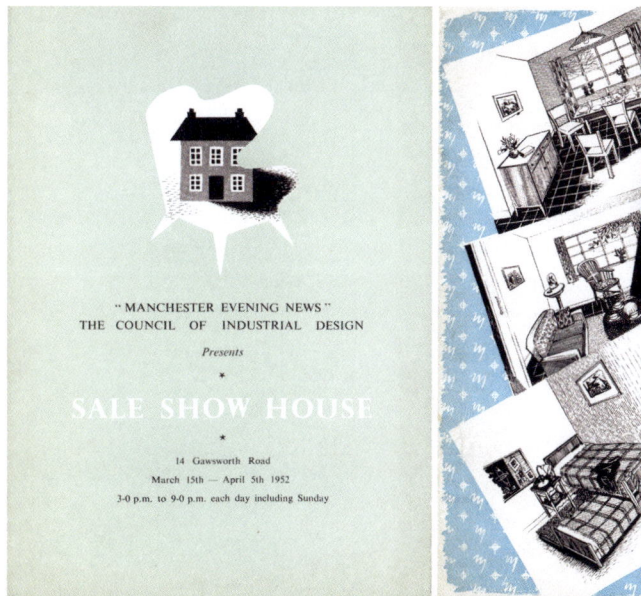

LEFT The distinctive design of the original Design Centre label, created by an in-house team

OPPOSITE Trade buyers making specialist use of the Design Index

In the coming months, five officers made 600 industrial visits, and forty per cent more manufacturers requested introductions to designers than in the previous twelve months, which had itself been a record year.[16] Their projects also appeared more ambitious.[17] In 1957, the Scottish Committee's premises at 46 West George Street, Glasgow, opened.

Under the banner 'Designs of the Year', twelve products were chosen for special recognition from among those shown during the Centre's first twelve months. To preserve objectivity, five panellists were proposed by the Faculty of Royal Designers for Industry, and the long-running award series commenced. The Duke of Edinburgh was invited to return for the ceremony, leading to a fruitful fifty-year-long collaboration. From that point on, his presence constituted a focal point for the Council's annual cycle of activities. In 1959, an overall winner became eligible for a prize he inaugurated, the Duke of Edinburgh's Prize for Elegant Design, which went to Charles Longman's Prestcold Packaway Refrigerator for the Pressed Steel Company.

The 1958 display season featured various prototypes, stimulating new products while fostering sales of existing ones. That autumn, the 'first provincial Design Centre exhibition' was staged at Bainbridge's of Newcastle upon Tyne, where an astonishing 50,000 visitors came in twenty-four days.[18] More followed. Over a thousand retailers received quarterly newsletters identifying items being shown in the Design Index or included in exhibitions.[19] Retailers and Centre visitors foresaw the usefulness of a distinguishing feature, and the emblematic, quartered, black-and-white triangle denoting Council approval was created by the Centre's in-house team.[20] Launched in autumn 1958, three million labels were ordered by nearly 300 manufacturers within six months.[21]

Review committees made up of four independent members, Council members in rotation, industrial officers and technical advisors met twice weekly to process Design Index (formerly Review) submissions. Very quickly, ten times more products were recorded by photograph or sample than could be shown at any one time in the Centre, creating a valuable adjunct.[22] During periods

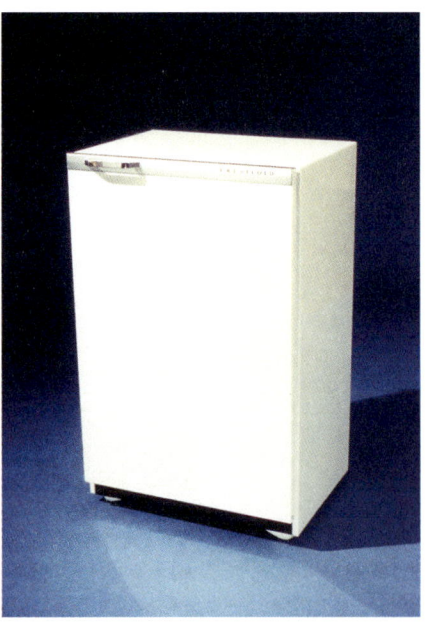

ABOVE C. W. F. Longman and E. G. M. Wilkes, Prestcold Packaway D301 refrigerator, 1959. Designed for the Prestcold Division of Pressed Steel Co. Ltd, it was the first recipient of the Duke of Edinburgh's Prize for Elegant Design

of display, companies paid from two shillings and six pence to ten shillings a day, according to dimensions.[23] Morning access was reserved for trade and professional enquirers. Innumerable trade bodies co-sponsored residential training for members whose interest they fostered through group visits to the Centre. These courses were well supported and frequently overbooked.[24] Vast quantities of photographic prints were generated and circulated to support journalism, commentary and education.[25] The Centre became a factory turning out current design information, for consumption by a wide variety of media, including broadcast and national press.

This decade saw the Council honing and sharpening the impact of its various activities, so that its 'earned income reached forty-five per cent of its total expenditure',[26] and hovered thereabouts for the next few decades. By spring 1959, the annual cycle for seven officers working in the field involved nearly 900 visits to factories, showrooms and trade fairs.[27] Fifty-five per cent of 5,000 items submitted to the Design Index were accepted, and goods still in production were subject to weeding as standards evolved.[28] In 1959, the Council itself received special recognition for its 'national, social and educational' work from a distinguished international jury associated with the 'Compasso d'Oro', awarded by Italian department store La Rinascente.

1. The Festival has generated its own growing literature, for example Becky E. Conekin, *The Autobiography of a Nation: The 1951 Festival of Britain* (Manchester: Manchester University Press, 2003), and Harriet Atkinson, *The Festival of Britain: A Land and its People* (London: I.B. Tauris, 2012).
2. CoID, *Annual Report, 1948–49*, 2.
3. Afterwards the Society of Industrial Artists and Designers, now the Chartered Society of Designers.
4. CoID, *Annual Report, 1951–52*, 9.
5. CoID, *Annual Report, 1952–53*, 2.
6. CoID, *Annual Report, 1951–52*, 8.
7. CoID, *Annual Report, 1949–50*, 7.
8. ibid., 3.
9. CoID, *Annual Report, 1952–53*, 3. The Council took over this responsibility from the Royal Fine Art Commission and it quickly became an area of concerted activity. On the broader context, see Eleanor Herring, *Street Furniture Design: Contesting Modernism in Post-War Britain* (London: Bloomsbury, 2016).
10. CoID, *Annual Report, 1951–52*, 16.
11. CoID, *Annual Report, 1953–54*, 4–5.
12. CoID, *Annual Report, 1952–53*, 16.
13. CoID, *Annual Report, 1955–56*, 5.
14. CoID, *Annual Report, 1956–57*, 16–17.
15. ibid., 9.
16. ibid., 10.
17. ibid., 17.
18. CoID, *Annual Report, 1958–59*, 18.
19. CoID, *Annual Report, 1957–58*, 15.
20. CoID, *Annual Report, 1958–59*, 18.
21. ibid., 3.
22. At any one time 1,000 items typically appeared in the Centre, while the Design Index held details of 10,000 products. CoID, *Annual Report, 1959–60*, 14 and 20.
23. CoID, *Annual Report, 1956–57*, 8.
24. CoID, *Annual Report, 1958–59*, 19.
25. On the Council's use of photography, see 'A Backroom Service? The Photographic Library of the Council of Industrial Design, 1945–60', *Journal of Design History*, 13/1 (2000), 39–57.
26. CoID, *Annual Report, 1959–60*, 12.
27. CoID, *Annual Report, 1958–59*, 17.
28. ibid., 16.

Taste, Tradition and Transformation in Post-war Britain
Penny Sparke

The 1950s was a decade of dramatic change. It began in the spirit of democracy and reconstruction, of the welfare state and austerity (rationing did not fully disappear until 1954), and ended in one of growing affluence, increasing individualism and what Harry Hopkins has described as 'the development of an "American-style" mass market'.[1] The forces that underpinned that change came from both the top down and the bottom up, often with strong tensions developing between them.

While those bottom-up forces were rooted in a laissez-faire approach, the governmental agenda was carefully planned. Both the Labour government and the Conservative governments of, in turn, Winston Churchill, Anthony Eden and Harold Macmillan, which replaced Labour in late 1951, focused on post-war economic growth. That necessitated influencing consumer taste to stimulate the home market and, as a result, the international market. The question of public taste was, therefore, linked to fundamental government policy and the brief was given to the Council of Industrial Design to encourage people to engage with, and to purchase, 'good modern design'.

The government of 1950s Britain sought to enhance the cultural lives of its inhabitants in several ways. The Arts Council, for example, formed in 1946, was active during the 1950s, not only helping to fund the 1951 Festival of Britain but also, in 1955, the Royal Opera House and the Royal Court Theatre.[2] A new design culture was part of that 'powerful vision of a modern, democratic nation'.[3] Although it was embedded within the Board of Trade, the Council adopted a moral, high-cultural approach with the aim of spreading its message as widely as possible. To that end, it disseminated its message through popular magazines (the editor of *Woman*, Edith Blair, was a member of the Council board), TV programmes and show houses in new housing estates.

At the same time as the government was fulfilling its mission, bottom-up social change was taking place in the UK, resulting in the emergence, by the end of the decade, of a fully fledged popular culture, manifested in music, fashionable dress and other lifestyle accessories. The increasing affluence, especially of the working and lower middle classes of the British population, generated a new market for which taste was more about social aspiration and the fulfilment of desire than, as it was for the Council, the implementation of high-cultural values.

The model for the bottom-up forces was provided by American popular culture, expressed in, among other forms, ostentatious automobiles and rock-and-roll music, whereas top-down 'good design', manifested in 'well-designed' products and environments, looked to industrial design and decorative arts precedents in the Scandinavian countries and Italy. The coincidence of these two forces created a scenario in which the Council had to adopt some strong strategies to ensure that its mission was heard and understood.

The two forces met head on in 1951 at the Festival of Britain, held on the South Bank in London. The event was planned by the Labour government, led by Deputy Prime Minister Herbert Morrison, and key players included architect and interior designer Hugh Casson; industrial designer

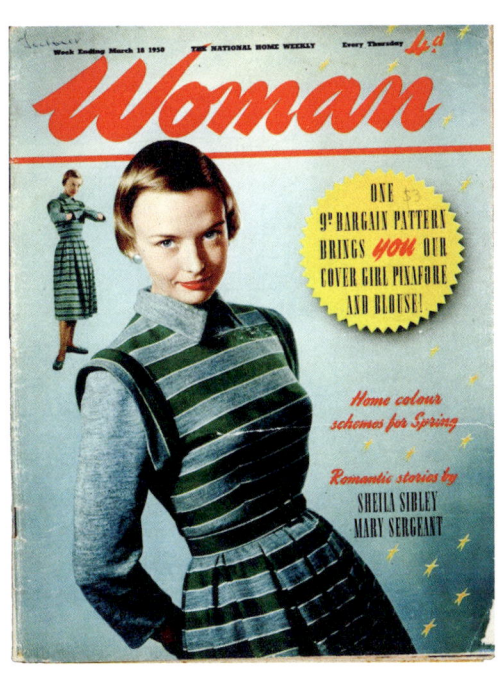

ABOVE Finn Juhl, Baker Sofa and Cocktail Table, 1951
LEFT *Woman* magazine, March 1950

ABOVE Homes and Gardens Pavilion, 1951. Festival of Britain exhibition building at South Bank, London

OPPOSITE Alison and Peter Smithson, House of the Future, 1956. Living room installation at the Daily Mail Ideal Home exhibition (left); Robin Day, 658 Chair, 1951. Plywood and tubular metal frame chair with upholstered seating, manufactured by S Hille & Co Ltd for the Royal Festival Hall (right)

OVERLEAF Douglas Scott, Routemaster Bus, 1956. View near Oxford Street. Photograph by Colin Tait

Misha Black; exhibition designers James Gardner and James Holland; the designer of the Dome of Discovery, architect Ralph Tubbs; and graphic designer Abram Games, who created the Festival of Britain symbol. The idea was that 'the people [were] giving themselves a pat on the back'.[4] The Council played a key role in the event, selecting all the exhibits for the 'Homes and Gardens' and the 'New Schools' sections. The overriding impact came from the bright colours and striking patterns that were on display. In the words of Hugh Casson, 'After ten years of austerity and drabness, people wanted the sensation of plenty.'[5] So thrilled was the public that it generated a fear on the part of the design establishment that the pendulum of public taste would swing too far in the opposite direction.

That popular commitment to the new aesthetic was demonstrated again in 1953, when the Design and Industries Association (DIA), formed back in 1915, organised the *Register Your Choice* exhibition at Charing Cross Underground Station. Two room settings were displayed – one in the modern idiom and the other in a popular, more traditional style. Sixty per cent of the people who registered their choice preferred the modern setting.[6]

The desire for a 'new look' was reinforced by the fact that many people were inhabiting the new houses that the government was building to offset earlier housing shortages. Churchill's Conservative government, with Macmillan heading the Ministry of Housing from 1951, built around 300,000 houses every year between 1953 and 1957.[7] Harry Hopkins explained, 'An England which had discarded Empire needed a new start inside the home also … a studied informality and flexibility were to be the new keynotes.'[8] Claiming that it had influenced the shift in taste, the Council proclaimed that 'not for a generation have so many people been interested in better design'.[9] In addition to the new privately owned housing, with open-plan, flexible interiors filled with products in what was described as the 'Contemporary' style, the government constructed public housing, new towns, civic centres and universities, all of which displayed what this author has described elsewhere as 'the rhetoric of modernism'.[10]

Cheryl Buckley has explained that 'the home provided the space where the post-war modernist vision of a better world was best articulated.'[11] Nowhere was that more in evidence than at the annual Ideal Home exhibitions hosted by the *Daily Mail*, which (having been initiated in 1908) ran throughout the 1950s, encouraging consumers to buy the new products and engage with the new, modern lifestyle.

The Council was part of a larger, longer-standing support system for design that continued into the 1950s. In addition to the DIA, the British Society of Industrial Artists, formed in 1930, was 'set up to look after the interest of designers and it was particularly keen to develop design as a legitimate vocation'.[12] The Royal Designers for Industry (RDI) scheme, established in 1936 by the Royal Society for the Encouragement of Arts, Manufactures and Commerce, 'was one of a number of initiatives in the interwar years to raise the status of the industrial design profession in Britain'. Robin Day, one of Britain's leading furniture designers, became an RDI in 1959.[13]

The strategic thrust of the Council was to ensure that 'good modern design' prevailed. It was thus important to train designers in a way that prepared them to work with

manufacturing industry, to encourage manufacturers to engage with professional designers and to ensure that consumers had access to designed goods. Buckley argues that, to fulfil these objectives, 'a new type of industrial designer was needed and to that end British art and design education renewed its offering.'[14] Under the leadership of Robin Darwin, who joined the institution in 1948, the Royal College of Art (RCA), which had been formed back in 1837, was restructured into a number of new schools: Graphic Design (led by Richard Guyatt, a key figure in design education); Engineering and Furniture Design (led by Dick Russell, known for modern industrial design); Textile Design; Ceramics; Silversmithing and Jewellery Design; and Fashion Design (led by Madge Garland, instrumental in shaping fashion education).[15] New staff with industry experience were invited to work there. Several students who graduated from the RCA in the 1950s went on to become leading figures through the decade. Among them were the furniture designer Robin Day who designed, among other iconic chairs, the 658 moulded plywood armchair created for the Royal Festival Hall, and – with his wife, textile designer Lucienne Day – a modern interior for the 1954 Milan Triennale; furniture and lighting designer Robert Heritage; furniture designer Ronald Carter, who went on to teach at the RCA himself; and designers Robert Welch and David Mellor. William Johnstone joined the Central School of Arts and Crafts in 1947 and quickly renewed the curriculum at that institution, adding 'basic design' to it.[16]

While many of the highly regarded 1950s modernist furniture designers graduated from the reformed art schools, others emerged from within industry itself. The Italian designer Lucian Ercolani, for example, set up his own furniture manufacturing company, Ercol, in the late 1940s. Based on traditional Windsor chairs, his products were adapted to suit the modern mood. Another designer-manufacturer, Ernest Race, established his own firm, Ernest Race Ltd, at the end of World War II. His much-loved steel-rod Antelope and Springbok chairs were admired at the Festival of Britain. Other furniture manufacturer and designer partnerships included those of Kandya and Danish designer Carl Jacobs, who created the elegant plywood Jason chair of 1950; Hille and Robin Day; Archie Shine and Robert Heritage; and Rotaflex and John and Sylvia Reid, who created some memorable modern lights together. (The couple also worked for Stag Furniture, designing a highly accessible range called Cumberland.) The manufacturer and professional designer team proved a highly successful formula, leading to the emergence of some classic modern furniture designs that were given Council approval.

In the hands of professional designers, what were formerly known as the domestic decorative arts – textiles, ceramics, glassware and metalwork – were given the 'modern' treatment as well. Lucienne Day, Althea McNish and Jacqueline Groag emerged as key figures in the textiles field, while Heal's Fabrics (for which Lucienne Day created her highly successful textile Calyx) and David Whitehead & Sons Ltd came to the fore as important manufacturers in that area; popular ceramic items were designed by, among others, the Midwinter company with Jessie Tait – her Primavera appeared in 1954 – and Terence Conran – creating Plant Life in 1957; Whitefriars Glass produced some striking modern designs by Geoffrey Baxter;[17] while,

LEFT   Lucian Ercolani, Butterfly Chair, 1956
ABOVE   Terence Conran, Plant Life, c.1955. Ceramic plate in 'Fashion' shape, manufactured by Midwinter

RIGHT Lucienne Day, Calyx, 1951. Printed textile manufactured by Heal & Son Ltd

in the field of metalwork, David Mellor created a strikingly modern cutlery set called Pride in 1959, and Robert Welch designed the elegant Campden candelabra in 1957 for J & J Wiggin Ltd. 'Good design' even extended its reach to engineered products: Douglas Scott's Routemaster bus received high praise, and Alec Issigonis's hugely innovative Mini automobile emerged right at the end of the decade.

While not all levels of society embraced modernity as enthusiastically as the new middle classes – the aristocratic world of country houses preferred the neo-traditional proposals of interior decorator John Fowler, and the viewers (many of them by means of their newly acquired television sets) of the 1953 coronation of Queen Elizabeth II revelled in the importance of the past – it is nonetheless true to say that the 1950s saw British society accept modern design on an unprecedented scale. To a significant degree, the top-down push to ensure that occurred in a morally and aesthetically appropriate manner was largely successful. In the following decade, however, the embrace of popular culture, the new affluence and the emphasis on youth that had begun to emerge in the late 1950s rose to new levels, challenging the design establishment to reassess its values and position.

1   Harry Hopkins, *The New Look: A Social History of the Forties and Fifties* (London: Secker & Warburg, 1964), 313.
2   'Our history: 1950s | Arts Council England', www.artscouncil.org.uk/our-organisation/our-history#t-in-page-nav-3, accessed 17 July 2024.
3   Christopher Breward and Ghislaine Wood, 'Tradition and Modernity 1945-79', in Christopher Breward and Ghislaine Wood (eds), *British Design from 1948: Innovation in the Modern Age* (London: V&A Publishing, 2012), 31.
4   Peter Lewis, *The 50s* (London: Book Club Associates, 1978), 11.
5   Penny Sparke, *Design in Context* (London: Quarto, 1987), 62.
6   'Design and Industries Association – Oxford Reference', www.oxfordreference.com/display/10.1093/oi/authority.20110803095712859, accessed 17 July 2024.
7   Cheryl Buckley, *Designing Modern Britain* (London: Reaktion Books, 2007), 131.
8   Hopkins, *The New Look*, 329.
9   ibid., 335.
10 Penny Sparke, 'At Home with Modernity: The New Domestic Scene', in Breward and Wood (eds.), *British Design from 1948*, 121.
11 Buckley, *Designing Modern Britain*, 141.
12 'Society of Industrial Artists and Designers | Artist Biographies', www.artbiogs.co.uk/2/societies/society-industrial-artists-designers, accessed 18 July 2024.
13 'Royal Designers for Industry – Oxford Reference', www.oxfordreference.com/display/10.1093/oi/authority.20110803100431517, accessed 17 July 2024.
14 Buckley, *Designing Modern Britain*, 138.
15 ibid.
16 ibid., 140.
17 'Geoffrey Baxter: A Glass Designer Whose Work Defines an Era – World Collectors Net', www.worldcollectorsnet.com/articles/geoffrey-baxter-a-glass-designer-whose-work-defines-an-era/#google_vignette, accessed 19 July 2024.

BELOW David Mellor and Robert Welch, Campden Cutlery, 1956. Stainless-steel flatware manufactured by Oneida (top); Ernest Race, Armchair, 1952. Plywood shell chair with foam-rubber cushioning (bottom)

ABOVE John and Sylvia Reid, Pendant Lamps, 1957. Cellulose acetate lighting awarded the Council's Design of the Year

LIBERTY.

OPPOSITE Meteor, 1956

Meteor
A Bold New Vision for Mid-century Modernism

First created in 1956, Meteor captures the optimism of the 1950s with its striking, angular and graphic forms. The design's sleek, bright and bold geometric stars evoke a sense of boundless possibility, inspired by the excitement felt at the time about space exploration and rapid technological progress.

Following the rise of mid-century modernism, Liberty's 1950s designs ventured into avant-garde territory, introducing a fresh visual language that departed from traditional styles. Influenced by artists such as Henri Matisse and Paul Klee, as well as the kinetic mobiles of Alexander Calder, Liberty designers began exploring bold, two-dimensional graphics. Patterns became vivid and abstract, with spiky molecular forms, streamlined shapes and linear compositions. This new approach fostered a dynamic, experimental aesthetic – one that harmonised futuristic sensibilities with an unmistakably modern vision.

The 1960s

Design on the World Stage

A Door Wide Open: The Design Council at Home and Abroad
Lesley Whitworth

By January 1960, interest in visiting the Design Centre warranted further extension of late-night openings. Initially Thursdays until 7 p.m., it became Thursdays and Wednesdays till 7 p.m. (in 1958), and finally both days until 9 p.m. This supplemented standard Saturday opening and enabled it to welcome a 'significant new audience of married and engaged couples'.[1] The Centre attained destination status with the publication of well-received souvenir books in 1961 and 1962. Meanwhile, the Scottish Design Centre's physical extension was opened by Gordon Russell, a Council life-member since departing as director.[2] It now hosted a copy of the Design Index reference source, and a second duplicate was destined for the Bristol Building Centre. In quick succession, the Midland Design and Building Centre, Nottingham, and the Manchester Building Centre both sought their own copies. An innovative ten-guinea 'pattern book' for retailers wanting to build versatile display units for approved stock, on the model of the Design Centre's own, was also launched. Twenty-one of them took advantage in the scheme's first year, multiplying the number of Design Council outposts in regional population centres. In a single year, civic and education authorities made an additional eighty-six sites available for Council publicity and posters, further enhancing visibility.[3] Princess Margaret's consort, Antony Armstrong-Jones,[4] began a long association with the Council, bringing it to the attention of royal well-wishers. Several industrial tours of Wales followed for this ambassador of Welsh extraction, informing a groundswell of feeling that it needed its own Design Council presence.

A third international congress, 'Design Policy for Corporate Buying' (1961), spanned hotels, hospitals,[5] transport concerns, schools, universities, industrial and commercial undertakings, and government agencies. The famous French-American industrial designer Raymond Loewy was exceptionally complimentary about the event.[6] A new post working with large-scale buyers was created and a well-regarded series of contract catalogues – Design Index excerpts – entered production, supported by the manufacturers that were featured in them.[7] Only fifty per cent of goods put forward for the Design Index succeeded

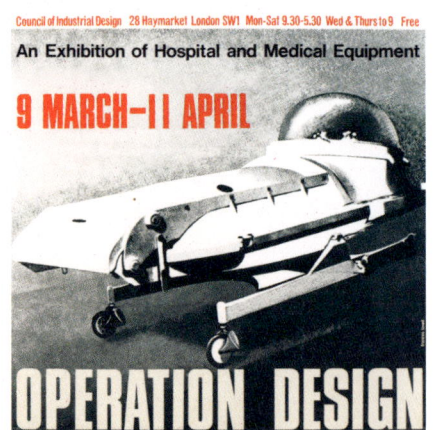

ABOVE *Operation Design: Hospitals for Today and Tomorrow* exhibition poster. Promotional material for Design Centre medical exhibition, 1966

PREVIOUS PAGE Malcolm Sayer, Jaguar E-type 1961. Sir William Lyons presents the car to the world's motoring press in Geneva on 15 March 1961 at the Parc des Eaux Vives

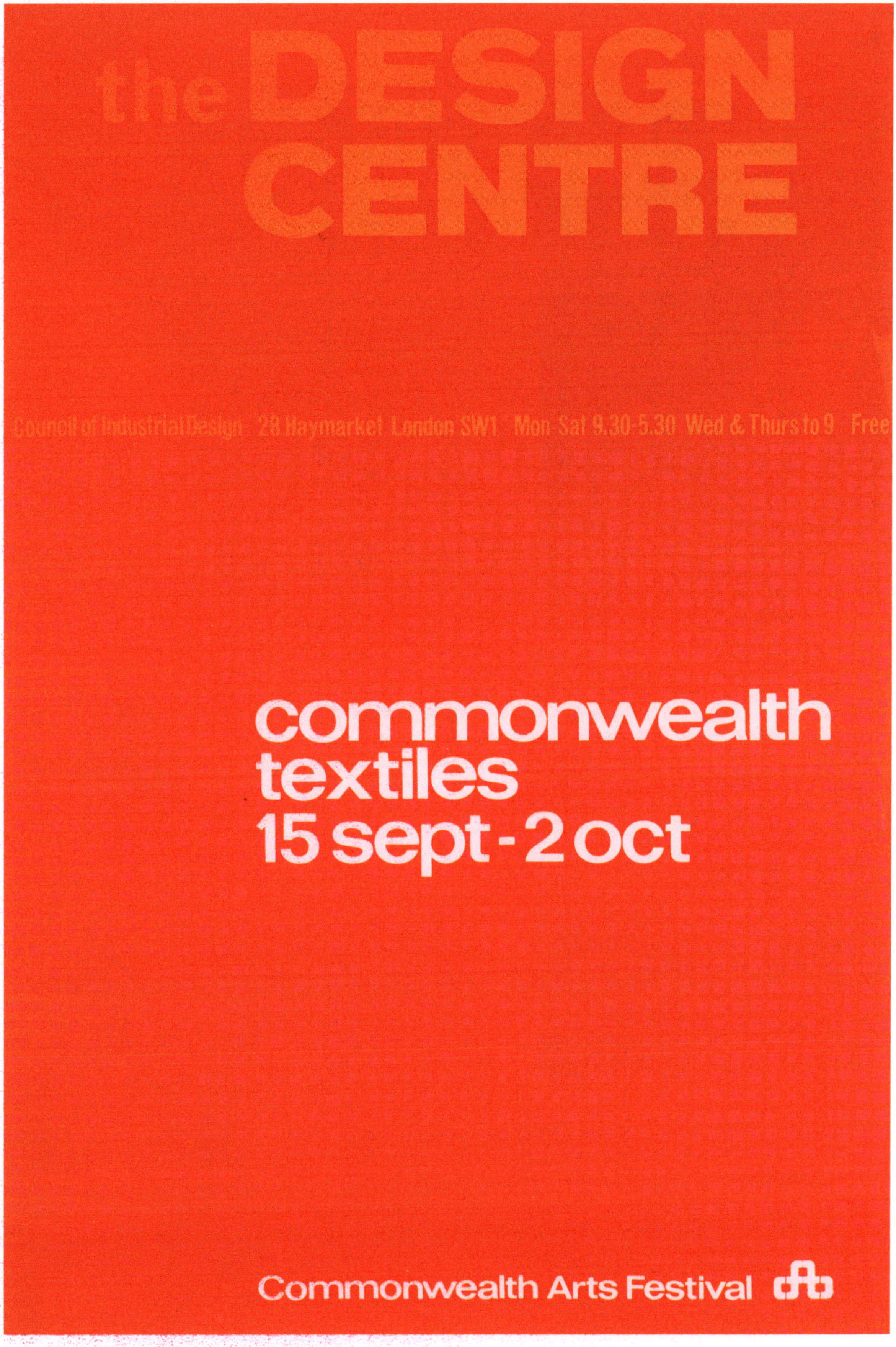

ABOVE *Commonwealth Textiles* exhibition poster. Promotional material for display in the newly created Mezzanine space. Design Centre, London, 1965

LEFT — Design Index poster, c.1960s. Material encouraging use of the index

ABOVE — Literature accompanying the Council's exhibition *The Role of the Industrial Designer in British Industry*, Moscow, 1964

RIGHT — Roger Dean, Sea Urchin Chair, 1967. Prototype furniture exhibited at the Design Centre

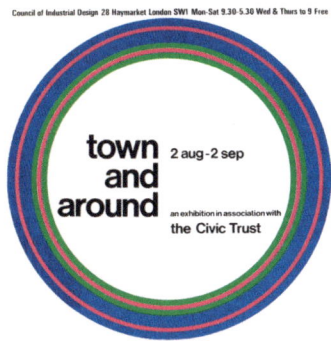

in 1961, but three years later this hit sixty per cent, with more submissions, through officers' consistent engagement with industry.[8] In 1961, fewer than 500 British companies were acting on their right to attach Design Centre labels to certain goods before they left the factory, but by 1968 this was 1,500.[9] Between 1968 and 1969, the total number of labels sold to manufacturers jumped by twenty-seven per cent to 11.5 million.[10]

This decade saw a proliferation of Council advisory committees,[11] and their contribution to external deliberations influenced choices concerning swathes of the material environment: hospitals, public services, accommodation, postage stamps, farm buildings, retail spaces, urban locations, railways, airports, government offices and British embassies.[12] The Institute of Directors invited the Council to cooperate on a report on 'Better Offices' (1961), the Leverhulme Trust asked the Council to administer its new Student Award for Industrial Design (Engineering), and Sainsbury's held its centenary exhibition at the Design Centre in 1969.[13] Allies were everywhere. After much delicate negotiation with the All-Union Scientific Research Institute for Industrial Design in Moscow, an exhibition was held there on the theme of 'The Role of the Industrial Designer in British Industry'.[14] Examples of bodies with which the Council was regularly in contact included, on one side, the Ministry of Technology, British Productivity Council and National Council for Quality and Reliability, and, on the other, the Consumer Advisory Council, the Consumers' Association (*Which?*) and Retail Trading Standards.[15] In the last-named case, a joint committee was formed to identify trends in complaints and consider what joint action might be taken. It was noticeable that during the tenure of a Labour government it was possible to use more expansive language about design: the Council could speak of its 'long-term contribution to the national economy and social welfare'.[16]

The Council worked closely with Training Boards for Furniture and Timber, Carpet, Distribution, Engineering, and Construction to help fill a vacuum in training places created by the government's 1964 Industrial Training Act. It 'would have been inexcusable not to have taken advantage of this new situation on behalf of design'.[17] Following the Crafts Centre of Great Britain's loss of government

ABOVE   Civic Trust poster. Promotional material for collaborative exhibition with the Civic Trust, 1967 (top); P. E. Pizzey and H. G. Davies, Urban Bollards, 1969. Range of lighted bollards manufactured by Frederick Thomas & Co. Ltd. Recognised in the Consumer Goods section of the Design Centre Awards (bottom)

RIGHT   *Additions to the Family* exhibition poster. Promotional material for Design Centre exhibition on furnishings for young and old, 1962

LEFT — Pupils from Western County Secondary Girls' School, Middlesex, visiting the Design Centre, 1965

OPPOSITE — Douglas Scott, Public Telephone, 1963. Pay-on-answer coin-operated telephone manufactured by Associated Automation Ltd with the General Post Office (GPO). Recipient of the Council's Design Centre Award

grant, the Design Council conceived a synergetic display that the Board of Trade declined. A new mezzanine space with more conceptual offerings nevertheless attracted fresh audiences from the spring of 1965. It showed prototypes, student work, products that stretched the Council's remit, even occasionally foreign design work. The second Scottish Design Centre opened in St Vincent Street, Glasgow, in November 1968.[18]

Attendance records were repeatedly broken. On 27 February 1963, 6,200 people visited *New Design for British Railways*.[19] On an exceptional Easter Monday the following year, they came at the rate of a thousand an hour.[20] Across twelve months of 1967–68, the Design Centre received one million visitors for the first time.[21] The 1968 *QE2* exhibition broke attendance records both for a day (7,390 on the opening day) and a week (35,340) in the spring, and these were again broken in summer, when the new records were 9,279 and 37,833 respectively.[22]

Sales of *Design* topped 15,000 a month, and the September 1960 issue reached 100 pages for the first time, while exceptional increases in the amount of advertising being booked enabled a rate increase, which helped the Council's balance sheet.[23] In 1968, it was described as 'primarily for business management readers'.[24]

In 1969, the conference 'Design, Society and the Future' was co-hosted in London with the Society of Industrial Artists and Designers (SIAD) on behalf of the International Council of Societies of Industrial Design (ICSID). With the generous support of over 100 British companies, nearly 1,000 delegates from more than thirty countries were welcomed, and the accompanying exhibition featured work from twenty-two of them. In a year when international activity was suppressed because of preparations for ICSID IV, the Council still organised exhibitions that reached in excess of 350,000 visitors in Tokyo, Vienna, Gothenburg and Jablonec 'at the request of the Board of Trade and in conjunction with the Central Office of Information', with all that entailed in terms of liaison with hosting bodies, sponsors, manufacturers, shippers and display planners. It also signed off a range of publications; hosted the Council Awards; held seventeen

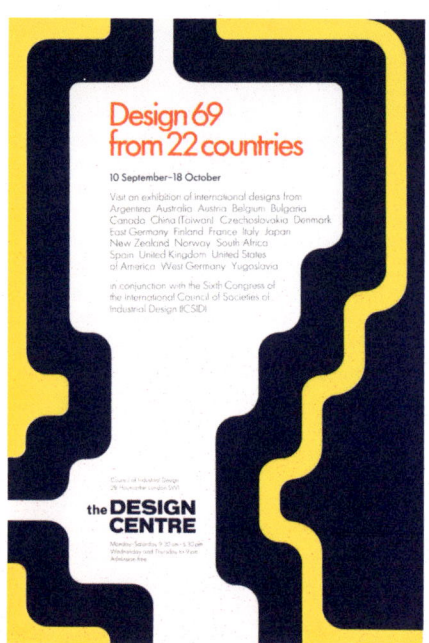

ABOVE — ICSID General Assembly poster. Promotional material for London exhibition co-hosted by the Council and SIAD, 1969

residential courses, five conferences and an international study tour; supported and administered the work of numerous Council selection panels and advisory committees; worked with consumer protection bodies; contributed to the judging and orchestration of various co-sponsored competitions; sent its industrial officers out in the field to visit quantities of firms and trade fairs; and welcomed an average of 3,800 visitors a day to the Design Centre.

During this decade when the Council self-described as 'government's chosen agent … spokesman and propagandist for design',[25] but remained sensible of a 'crust of suspicion and indifference' among its intended audience,[26] it observed the flattering emergence of equivalent national bodies, then feared being overtaken.[27] On 17 April 1969, the President of the Board of Trade announced the government's acceptance – in principle – of the recommendation of a Council of Engineering Institutions working party that engineering design could best be represented and promoted by a single body working across industrial and engineering design.

1   CoID, *Annual Report, 1959–60*, 14.
2   See Gordon Russell, *Designer's Trade: The Autobiography of Gordon Russell* (London: George Allen & Unwin, 1968).
3   The reporting year 1963–64. The Council had a negligible budget for promotion.
4   Afterwards Earl of Snowdon.
5   The Council took an interest in medical design long before it was adopted as an award category. See, for example, the special issue of *Design* 207, March 1966, 'Operation Design: Hospitals for Today and Tomorrow'.
6   CoID, *Annual Report, 1961–62*, 38.
7   For example, the first Contract Furniture catalogue appeared in 1964 (CoID, *Annual Report, 1964–65*, 8).
8   CoID, *Annual Report, 1960–61*, 10, and CoID, *Annual Report, 1963–64*, 11. On the general consumer context for the period, see Jennifer Harris, Sarah Hyde and Greg Smith, *1966 and All That: Design and the Consumer in Britain, 1960–69* (London: Trefoil, 1986).
9   CoID, *Annual Report, 1960–61*, 11, and CoID, *Annual Report, 1967–68*, 13.
10 CoID, *Annual Report, 1968–69*, 15.
11 It is possible to see these as the logical successors to the sectoral Design Centres envisaged in the 1940s.
12 Relevant bodies in these areas consulted the Record of Designers for recommendations. The resource was renamed Designer Selection Service later in the decade.
13 CoID, *Annual Report, 1960–61*, 31; CoID, *Annual Report, 1961–62*, 35; CoID, *Annual Report, 1969–70*, 12.
14 The Council also mounted displays in Warsaw, Krakow, Prague, Bratislava and Budapest between 1963 and 1966.
15 For a discussion of the emergence of consumer activism and a dedicated social movement, see Matthew Hilton, *Consumerism in Twentieth-Century Britain: The Search for a Historical Movement* (Cambridge: Cambridge University Press, 2003), especially Part II.
16 CoID, *Annual Report, 1966–67*, 4.
17 CoID, *Annual Report, 1969–70*, 4.
18 The lease on the previous premises in West George Street having come to an end.
19 Although primarily associated with railway closures in the popular memory, Dr Richard Beeching was also associated with a period of significant design investment at British Rail. This show celebrated the launch of its new corporate identity and logo.
20 CoID, *Annual Report, 1963–64*, 8.
21 CoID, *Annual Report, 1966–67*, 5, and CoID, *Annual Report, 1967–68*, 3 and 13.
22 CoID, Annual Report, 1967–68, 13, and CoID, *Annual Report, 1968–69*, 13.
23 CoID, *Annual Report, 1960–61*, 30.
24 CoID, *Annual Report, 1967–68*, 34.
25 CoID, *Annual Report, 1964–65*, 4.
26 CoID, *Annual Report, 1965–66*, 3.
27 CoID, *Annual Report, 1963–64*, 4; here it refers to the Belgian Design Centre, opened in February 1964, as its 'youngest relative'. On the Belgian case, see Katarina Serulus, *Design & Politics: The Public Promotion of Industrial Design in Postwar Belgium (1950–1986)* (Leuven: Leuven University Press, 2018).

Everything Changed, Everything Remains the Same: Remembering the Sixties
Christopher Breward

Of all the post-war design decades, the 1960s must surely have taken up the greatest proportion of paper, ink and celluloid in print and film – and commanded the most attention from design historians and the popular imagination over the intervening years.[1] The raw, hopeful power of 'the Sixties' as a signifier of change is almost tangible in its energy, and it is the products of British designers, manufacturers and cultural producers that stand out most starkly in the global lexicon of the period's most famous symbols. From Beatles record-cover designs by Peter Blake and Richard Hamilton, through Mary Quant's mini-dresses and Barbara Hulanicki's Biba boutiques, Alec Issigonis's Mini Cooper, Jaguar's E-Type sports car and Alex Moulton's 'Stowaway' bicycle, to Jock Kinneir and Margaret Calvert's motorway signage and Robin Day's polypropylene chairs – the sharp, playful clutter of the 'swinging' era's material and graphic clichés have furnished countless 'mod', 'op', 'pop' and psychedelic dreamscapes.

Objectively speaking, as a child born in 1965, my own memories of the decade's second half, though faint and limited, are as evocative as the familiar stereotypes, but perhaps a little more prosaic. I was born in student digs in Bristol, weaned in South Gloucestershire, and set out to nursery and infant schools in North Kent, with the experiences of my family miles from the milieu of Soho and Chelsea – as were most people's. But in many ways the physical environment of those formative years, as I remember it, is as indicative of the rapidly changing political, economic and social context of the times as any glamorous Habitat or Biba store window and catalogue.

The Clifton flat to which my parents brought me home from maternity hospital was dark, damp and Victorian, but optimistically furnished with a rubber plant and a G Plan coffee table. As a student of aeronautical engineering and an assistant computer operator at the Rolls-Royce factory in Filton, my newly married parents were, unknowingly, at the searing edge of Harold Wilson's 'white heat' of technology (that clarion call for science and progress made by the future prime minister at the 1963 Labour Conference, before the party was elected to government the following year). As my father's graduate search for employment took us further afield, we lived in 'Span'-like new 'executive' homes in Thornbury and Westerham. For the entertainment of family and friends, I willingly danced to Lulu's Eurovision hit 'Boom Bang-a-Bang', played on the Dansette record player or flickering in black and white on the rented Rediffusion television. And, in a reminder that the 1940s and '50s were not so far behind, I remember the unveiling on Westerham Village Green in 1969 of the memorial statue of the late Winston Churchill, a hulking gorilla-like homunculus glowering over a new world, gifted by the Yugoslavian people in one of those cultural détentes that marked the softer side of the Cold War. In a nod to the future, a photograph taken on my father's Kenneth Grange-designed Brownie Vecta camera records the junior me, in a red Courtaulds 'Ladybird' anorak, swinging my legs on a wall above the Severn suspension bridge, opened by Queen Elizabeth II a couple of years before in 1966.

In retrospect, while that all seems miles away from the fashionable King's Road and Carnaby Street, or the serious

ABOVE   Peter Blake, album artwork for *Sergeant Pepper's Lonely Hearts Club Band*, 1967

reforming discourse of *Design* magazine, there are traces in those early material memories of the historical flows and pressures that produced the distinctive shapes and textures of British design in the 1960s. I recall the late and much-missed design historian Gillian Naylor, who worked as a journalist at *Design* in the late 1950s and early '60s, and two decades later taught me at the Royal College of Art, telling our class, with a draw on her cigarette and much nostalgia and hilarity, what she spent her *Design* pay packets on. I'm hazy on the detail – it may have involved a saxophone, a Mary Quant dress and a Mini Cooper – but in a similar vein it evoked more than the sum of its parts in its evocation of hope, change and newness.[2]

The articles and features of *Design* itself provide a more 'purist' account of the design establishment's attempts to keep pace with rapid industrial and policy advances, and indeed set standards for design education and consumer taste. A random selection of the stand-out keywords and phrases in consecutive issues from 1960 to 1969 provides a window into the preoccupations and shifting fortunes of Britain's design ecology. Topics covered over the period included: 'Moscow Consumer Goods', 'The Ergonomics Research Society', 'Human Factors in Healing', 'Details from Coventry Cathedral', 'National Productivity Year', 'Street Furniture Panel', 'French Design: Common Market Review', 'British Railways', 'General Post Office', 'Overhead Power Lines', 'Milan Triennale', 'Enterprise Scotland', 'Art Nouveau', 'Art Schools Under Scrutiny', 'Designing By Making', 'British Poster Awards', 'Eating Out Can Be Fun', 'A City Is Not A Tree', 'What About the Office Workers?', 'Behind the Scene: Carnaby Street', 'Signs of the Times at Glasgow Airport', 'Furniture for the Primary School', 'Do It Yourself Dinghy', 'Toys and Toymakers', 'The Sit-Ins and Beyond', 'Zap! Pow! Zowie!' and 'QE2'.

The whole contradictory mess of a society in violent transition is there in those words and images, evoking the shift from a paternalistic, technocratic and controlled post-war status quo to social and economic revolution and the emergence of a counterculture for whom 'control' was anathema. In a significant *Design* article of March 1968 titled 'Cold Rice Pudding and Revisionism', Christopher Cornford provides a compelling summary of the existential factors that were changing the language, appearance and meaning of contemporary material and visual culture forever. These included:

> [T]he advent of automation; the proliferation of new materials which have no craft tradition either to follow or depart from; the formal implications of space age technology; the teenage revolution and the rise of a new patronage; the dominance of anti-art, neo-Dada and Pop tendencies; the ferocious assault on good taste; the rise of 'environmental design'; the revival of art nouveau, not as fad but as vitamin; the advent of the computer as design tool; the need for a new anthropology of Western man, a new set of values: what are we?[3]

What are we, indeed! If 1960s Britain and its design values can be characterised as anything, then this questioning stance must count as a defining element, encapsulated most clearly in the schisms that emerged in the theory and governance of education in British art and design schools

RIGHT   Biba, the trendy Kensington department store run by Barbara Hulanicki with her husband, Stephen Fitz-Simon, London, 1966

OPPOSITE   Mary Quant at her drawing table in her home in Draycott Place, Chelsea, London, sketching designs, 1966

OPPOSITE Breward family photograph of Severn Suspension Bridge, 1969 (top); Kenneth Grange, Vecta Brownie Camera, 1963. Recipient of the Council's Design Centre Award in 1964 (bottom)

ABOVE Alex Moulton, Moulton Stowaway Bicycle, 1964. Recipient of the Council's Design Centre Award

LEFT *Design* magazine, August 1966
BELOW Tony Carey, Hornsey College of Art protest poster, May–June 1968

during the period. Concerns about the training of artists and designers in British art schools had been growing since the late 1940s. Politicians, higher-education leaders and industrialists were variously unhappy with outdated curricula that were failing to keep up with advances in technology or economic need, the nationwide provision of colleges, the level of qualifications awarded, and more philosophical matters concerning the social role of the arts and value hierarchies between fine art, applied design and theory. In 1959, William Coldstream – artist and principal of the Slade School of Art – was appointed by the government to chair the National Advisory Council of Art Education Committee with a view to reforming the whole system. The Committee published its first report, known as the 'Coldstream Report', in 1960. Its recommendations included the introduction of multidisciplinary, pre-diploma 'foundation' courses covering fine art, graphic design, craft and textiles, and fashion, and providing compulsory lectures in the history of art and complementary (contextual) studies.

The following year, the independent National Council for Diplomas in Art and Design was established under the leadership of architectural historian John Summerson to set rigorous national standards by which individual art schools would be assessed. In 1964, the Summerson Committee reported on its assessments, which considered that only 61 of 201 courses submitted by 72 colleges across the country met its criteria for awarding the National Diploma in Design. Those that failed were advised to focus on vocational technical courses for the design trades. The path to progress and reform was a rocky one, but the debate planted seeds that would eventually result in a unique flowering of art and design education in the UK, which flourished through to the first decade of the twenty-first century.[4]

Coldstream and Summerson were establishment types of the class (upper middle) and generation (pre-war) whose patrician views became increasingly outmoded as the decade matured. By 1968, resistance to the Old World position they occupied exploded in the student-led protests that rocked universities across Europe and the United States. In Britain, the fervour of revolution had a particular art-and-design-school flavour, encapsulated by the sit-in at Hornsey College of Art. Here, students rejected the authority of the diploma and the social divisions it represented and called for an anti-system approach informed by Marxist radicalism and avant-garde aesthetic sensibilities (of the kind espoused by Cornford's essay in *Design* of the same year). Most importantly, the drama that played out in a quiet North London suburb had much wider significance and was repeated in many other art schools and contexts, marking the late 1960s as a moment when the big questions around what art is and who it is for, and whether design was in the service of consumerism or a tool for saving a broken world, entered the national conversation for the first time.[5]

It is perhaps easy when looking back to the 1960s to be swayed by the bright lights of its design archetypes – it is undeniably fun to be swayed, too! I get great pleasure from turning the pages of *Time* magazine's iconic April 1966 issue, given over to 'London: The Swinging City' and graced by Geoffrey Dickinson's memorable cover illustration. Here, all that we find distinctive about the decade is recorded: Big

64

Ben, a Routemaster bus and a suburban bingo hall stand in for quirky tradition and a reappraisal of the vernacular as 'camp'; the neon cinema sign advertising the Michael Caine vehicle *Alfie* conjures up Cilla Black's theme song; modernist road signs; that E-Type Jag and a Mini Cooper signify modernity, with a Rolls-Royce thrown in for 'high and low' contrast alongside a roulette table. In the door of a discotheque, a fashion photographer mimics David Hemming's approximation of David Bailey in Antonioni's movie *Blow-Up* of the same year, aiming his camera at a member of The Who, a 'dolly bird' in an op-art dress and even Prime Minister Wilson in his Gannex raincoat waving a Union Jack flag. But behind the throwaway carnival iconography lies something more profound and enduring – yet also elusive.[6]

David Bailey himself tried to capture that legacy in the elegiac book *Goodbye Baby and Amen* that he co-authored with Peter Evans in 1969, which immortalised in images and words a metropolitan clique of fashion models, actors, filmmakers, designers, restaurateurs, musicians and artists who had helped to make Britain swing. 'It will be a little time yet', they stated in their conclusion, 'before the writers and sociologists … get the age pinned down beneath the seismograph needles and make patterns that are not merely pretty, but enlightening. Meanwhile we shall recall it with pleasure and fury and some sadness too.'[7]

Sixty years on, it is still with a mix of wistful nostalgia, haunting recognition and prescient hindsight that we look back on the decade's contribution to the landscape we inhabit now. It was a war in the Middle East and an ensuing oil crisis that brought the good times to a halt then. Cold War with the former USSR and China propelled many of the cultural and technological advances that changed the art scene and industrial design in the West while intensifying its paranoia. Generations seemed as far apart as they had ever been in the clothes they wore, the values they held and their attitudes to authority or increased permissiveness. Famine in Africa, the extinction of wild animal species and poverty at home provoked anger, shame and a new spirit of social and charity campaigning, while an explosion of creativity in the advertising, television and mass-media worlds led consumers to question the veracity of the messages they were receiving. All of this remains familiar. The spirit of the Sixties still endures. Everything changed. Everything remains the same. My father's Brownie Vecta camera remains (now without its reel of film) in his study drawer. The Severn suspension bridge still reaches out towards Wales.

1   Cheryl Buckley, *Designing Modern Britain* (London: Reaktion Books, 2007); Mark Donnelly, *Sixties Britain* (Edinburgh: Pearson, 2005); David Jeremiah, *Architecture and Design for the Family in Britain, 1900–70* (Manchester: Manchester University Press, 2000); Simon Rycroft, *Swinging City: A Cultural Geography of London 1950–1974* (Farnham: Ashgate, 2011); Jonathan M. Woodham, *Twentieth-Century Design* (Oxford: Oxford University Press, 1997).
2   Gillian Naylor and Ken Garland, '*Design* magazine – a conversation', in Jeremy Aynsley and Kate Forde (eds.), *Design and the Modern Magazine* (Manchester: Manchester University Press, 2007), 156–76.
3   Christopher Cornford, 'Cold Rice Pudding and Revisionism', *Design* (March 1968).
4   Simon Martin, 'Pop Goes the Art School: Design and Education', in Christopher Breward and Ghislaine Wood (eds.), *British Design from 1948: Innovation in the Modern Age* (London: V&A Publishing, 2012), 172.
5   Lisa Tickner, *London's New Scene: Art and Culture in the 1960s* (New Haven and London: Paul Mellon Centre for Studies in British Art, 2020), 232–67.
6   Christopher Breward, David Gilbert and Jenny Lister (eds), *Swinging Sixties* (London: V&A Publishing, 2006), 8–21.
7   David Bailey and Peter Evans, *Goodbye Baby and Amen: A Saraband for the Sixties* (London: Corgi Books, 1969), 237.

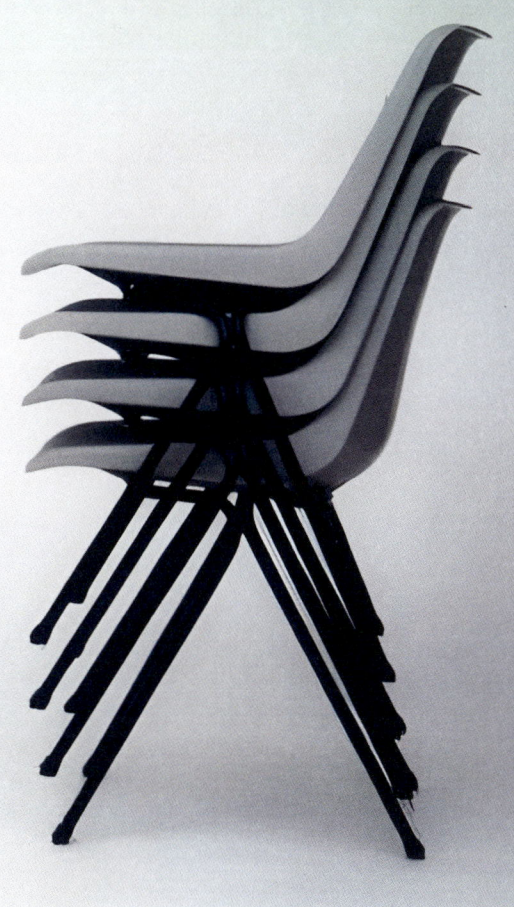

OPPOSITE   Margaret Calvert and Jock Kinneir, Children crossing sign for British roadways, 1957–67. Part of their pioneering redesign of the UK's road signage system, this pictogram replaced written warnings with a clear, modern visual language that improved legibility and set a new global standard for wayfinding

ABOVE   Robin Day, Polyprop Chair, 1964. Recipient of the Council's Design Centre Award in 1965, this lightweight, durable chair became one of the world's most successful mass-produced seating designs

68

LIBERTY.

OPPOSITE   Rosetti, 1910s, and Frieze, 1968

Rosetti & Frieze
The Art Nouveau Revival

A dramatic display of vibrant Art Nouveau poppies, Rosetti was created by the Silver Studio during the 1910s. The design is a stunning representation of the era's aesthetic, characterised by oversized flowers, meandering silhouettes, bold outlines and graceful swirls.

An archival classic, Frieze was originally created in 1968 by the famous British designer – and Liberty's Design Director at the time – Bernard Nevill. A revival of traditional Art Nouveau landscape prints, this beautifully hand-painted panorama showcases subtly arranged clusters of stylised trees, set in a dreamy, jewel-toned setting.

Art Nouveau, with its flowing lines and inspiration from nature, had been central to Liberty's identity since the 1890s. In the 1960s, the design house revived its celebrated motifs for the 'Swinging Sixties' market, introducing bold patterns influenced by Vorticism. These vivid designs combined dramatic blooms, swirling geometrics and imagined landscapes, capturing the decade's vibrant energy while honouring Liberty's enduring legacy.

The 1970s

Design in Flux

Retrenchment and Renaissance: The Design Council in Transition
Lesley Whitworth

More than at any time since the 1940s, the 1970s was a decade when the Council seemed peculiarly at the mercy of government policy.[1]

Things started well, with ringing endorsements from Labour-appointed consultants following prolonged scrutiny: 'The organisation is efficient and well run. The enthusiasm of the staff at all levels is outstanding. In most of the Council's activities the benefits are measurably greater than the cost.'[2] However, in the summer of 1970, the incoming Conservatives paused any transition to a new National Design Council and committed instead to reviewing all industry-supporting services. Remarkably, Council member John Davies resigned on becoming MP for Knutsford and was then made Secretary of State for Trade and Industry – the Council's sponsoring department. The Council was favourably reviewed, yet asked to 'adjust their priorities' and reduce grant-dependence.[3] Messaging around 'social and environmental issues' receded,[4] and the emphasis moved to technologically sophisticated engineering products, whose export value was well understood.

Under Labour (1974–79), the National Economic Development Council's 'new industrial strategy' recentred on manufacturing, including a design-led recovery. During 1979, design was 'the subject of more intense and authoritative advocacy than at almost any previous time in the Council's history'.[5] The Corfield Report identified design as the means to improve both manufacturing[6] and competitive appeal; the Advisory Council for Applied Research and Development and a Department of Industry committee both examined the relationship between product development, competitiveness and industrial innovation; and the Department of Prices and Consumer Protection published a 'National Strategy for Quality'.[7] All regarded design as vital to attaining these ends. Yet meeting targets for new Design Index selections proved impossible late in the decade. Items remained in production that should have been superseded. The decade represented an unenviably bumpy ride.

Following years of professional and governmental deliberation, the Council of Industrial Design was officially renamed the Design Council on 1 April

ABOVE — *Furniture Takes to Technology* exhibition poster, 1973. This Design Centre exhibition featured the revolutionary injection-moulded polypropylene stacking chair designed by Robin Day for Hille Ltd

PREVIOUS PAGE — Jamie Reid, poster for the Sex Pistols' *God Save the Queen*, 1977

1972. This rebranding reflected the government's push to modernise British industry, strengthening the Council's role by integrating engineering expertise into its remit. Paul Reilly, director since 1960, remained at the helm, overseeing this transition as the Council adjusted to new expectations – albeit without additional funding. Ironically, recruiting a Head of Engineering Design only became possible through improved income from consumer goods' activities.[8] Some short-lived respite was followed by double-digit inflation, which made budget management exceptionally difficult for staff. There were two strategic responses.

After only a short time in operation, engineering-design field officers, who tended to be generalists but had recourse to the carefully assembled Record of Engineering Design Expertise,[9] were brought within a new Design Advisory Service accessed by subscription to recover costs.[10] The long-standing team working with the consumer and contract industries, who tended to be specialists, were also absorbed.[11]

Next, fees paid by companies when their Design Index products featured in displays ended, with Department of Industry consent, from 1978. Further improving its offer to manufacturers, the Design Centre's mezzanine was repurposed to retail domestic products. The new Marketing Services team also dealt with the iconic label. And there were other milestones: in November 1970, the Scottish Design Centre welcomed its 500,000th visitor,[12] and on St David's Day of 1974 the long-awaited Welsh Design Council office and showroom at Pearl Assurance House, Cardiff, welcomed its first. Despite the blackouts during that same year, Design Centre attendance increased by twenty-five per cent to almost 5,000 a day and continued to grow,[13] and 1974's *Tomorrow's World* exhibition attracted the highest-ever recorded visitor total (58,231) between 13 March and 6 April.[14] Other notable exhibitions included one marking the UK's admission to the European Economic Community (1 January 1973) with a display of European goods,[15] and *Enterprise and Innovation*, the largest ever held, marked the Centre's twenty-first birthday by showing the design policies and products of eighty diverse British companies. With an eye on contemporary preoccupations, *Here*

ABOVE   The Council's new logo was launched in 1977 (top); Poster for the Council's hugely popular 1974 exhibition, themed around the BBC's *Tomorrow's World* programme (bottom)

RIGHT   Display to celebrate the sale of the 100 millionth Council of Industrial Design Swingtag, 1970

OVERLEAF   The 1978 Ford Fiesta saloon was recognised among this decade's first tranche of award-winning vehicles

LEFT *Playing and Learning* exhibition poster, 1974. The Council's concern for child-centred design was long-standing (left); *Streets Ahead* exhibition poster, 1974 (right)

Today: An Exhibition of Products Designed for a Short Life and a celebration of plastics, both in 1970, seem dissonant.

The Council's publishing wing continued to flourish. The 1970–71 *Street Furniture Catalogue* 'broke all previous records in revenue and coverage', and a gift/souvenir catalogue was launched.[16] Retail training – reduced during preparations for decimalisation – was supported by new series for sales staff and buyers.[17] Curry's electrical retailers bought 40,000 *Hi-Fidelity* (audio system) leaflets for distribution to customers. *Design Calendar* and *Design Bulletin* were redesigned, and *Design*'s enquiry service received nearly 11,000 queries in its inaugural year. *A Management Guide to Corporate Identity,* based on three conferences and nine case studies, highlighted an emergent theme and sold over 2,000 copies. The Council also began to appear in the new weekend colour supplements. Sixteen synopses and three manuscripts on engineering design were quickly approved, with more following,[18] and the Council bought *Engineering* magazine from IPC in September 1973, turning it into a consistent award winner.[19] Letterpress lithography and a new layout improved *Design*'s appearance, with readership of both magazines exceeding 100,000.[20] New bookstalls and souvenir counters appeared in the London and Glasgow Design Centres: within five years they were Britain's premier source of publications on engineering, design, architecture and crafts, holding 2,000 titles and supporting a mail-order operation.[21] In one year, publishing income rose from £14,957 to £78,883.[22]

After seventeen years as director and twenty-nine with the Council, Paul Reilly retired in 1977,[23] the same year that North Sea oil revenues finally brought the country some relief.[24] The Council's Awards programme expanded its categories,[25] and a new series of the Duke of Edinburgh's Prize was inaugurated. The Council withdrew from involvement with the Poster Awards, but took on ever more responsibility for the administration of co-sponsored prizes such as the Molins Design Prize for diploma/degree students of engineering or engineering science.

ABOVE John McArthur, microscope by the Open University, 1972. McArthur was the recipient of one of two Duke of Edinburgh's Design Prizes that year

A new Schools Design prize proved highly newsworthy and indicated a new direction of travel.[26] The Council's first careers leaflet covering both industrial and engineering design appeared, plus another persuading graduates in both fields to teach. While the decade was punctuated by important reports on the training of design students and their employment opportunities,[27] a new sense of purpose was crystallising around the design education of school-age children and the teaching resources necessary to support that process,[28] in order that they 'gain a better understanding of the industrial society and the environment in which they live'.[29]

1. For a broader understanding of the first part of this decade, see Dominic Sandbrook, *State of Emergency – The Way We Were: Britain 1970–74* (London: Allen Lane, 2010).
2. Excerpt from report by John Hoskyns & Co. Ltd delivered to the Board of Trade and Ministry of Technology, 20 January 1970, cited in CoID, *Annual Report*, 1969–70, 3–4.
3. CoID, *Annual Report*, 1971–72, 2.
4. Ibid.
5. Design Council, *Annual Report*, 1978–79, 6.
6. National Economic Development Office, *Product Design (Report by KG Corfield)* (London: NEDO, 1979).
7. All cited in Design Council, *Annual Report*, 1978–79, 6.
8. CoID, *Annual Report*, 1971–72, 2, and Design Council, *Annual Report*, 1972–73, 1.
9. The Record was built up through contacts with universities, professional institutions, research associations, laboratories, government departments and nationalised industries to encompass a full sphere of specialist technical assistance.
10. The Council was encouraged by evidence already emerging of companies making substantial savings through increased efficiency after contact with its staff. Design Council, *Annual Report*, 1975–76, 5.
11. The Design Advisory Service launched in September 1976 and assumed its final form in 1978.
12. CoID, *Annual Report*, 1970–71, 18.
13. CoID, *Annual Report*, 1971–72, 2. By 1972–73, the average stood at 5,662.
14. Design Council, *Annual Report*, 1973–74, 11.
15. However, related increases in value-added tax (VAT) also harmed product development, and once the pound recovered its value after 1977, exporters lost an important price advantage and there were fears of an import boom.
16. CoID, *Annual Report*, 1969–70, 4, and Design Council, *Annual Report*, 1973–74, 22.
17. UK Decimal Day, which banished pounds, shillings and pennies, was 15 February 1971.
18. These were published by Oxford University Press in association with the British Standards Institute and the Council of Engineering Institions. By 1976, there were ten guides available with forty-two at different stages of planning, and nearly 30,000 had been sold. Design Council, *Annual Report*, 1975–76, 23.
19. Independent readership surveys also confirmed *Engineering* as the leading publication for engineers and engineering manufacturers. See Design Council, *Annual Report*, 1978–79, 12; and Design Council, *Annual Report*, 1979–80, 4.
20. Design Council, *Annual Review*, 1978–79, 12.
21. CoID, *Annual Report*, 1971–72, 2, and Design Council, *Annual Report*, 1976–77, 13.
22. Design Council, *Annual Report*, 1976–77, 15–16.
23. See Paul Reilly, *An Eye for Design: An Autobiography* (London: Max Reinhardt, 1987).
24. Although the pound's improving value from autumn 1977 meant the loss of an important price advantage for exporters and once more the fear of an import boom.
25. A category for Medical Equipment was added to the Design Council Awards in 1972, in association with the King Edward's Hospital Fund for London and the Department of Health and Social Security. A further announcement in September 1973 co-sponsored by the Society of Motor Manufacturers and Traders immediately attracted over eighty submissions, from complete vehicles to individual components. On the evolution of the Council's award programme, see Lily Crowther, *Award-Winning British Design, 1957–1988* (London: V&A Publishing, 2012).
26. Ten prizes to the value of £1,250 were awarded for the design of useful objects, incorporating technical and aesthetic aspects. The first winners were announced in autumn 1977. Design Council, *Annual Report*, 1976–77, 10.
27. The Council's Design Education Study Group produced a report on 'Engineering Design Education' in 1976 and one on 'Industrial Design Education in the UK' in 1977. The Department of Education and Science produced one on 'The Employment of Art College Leavers' in 1972, about which see John Blake and Michael Kitson, 'Lessons for Design Educators', *Design* (October 1972), 62–63.
28. On the Council's earliest engagement with school-age children, see Jane Pavitt (ed.) *Camberwell Collection* (London: Camberwell College of Arts, 1996).
29. Preliminary report of the Secondary Education Working Party, cited in Design Council, *Annual Report*, 1978–79, 9.

Promotion, Professionalisation and Protest in British Design
Jonathan M. Woodham

In 1970, manufacturing industry represented the largest sector of the British economy (thirty per cent), although by the end of the decade it had fallen to twenty-three per cent.[1] An increasingly 'missing' feature of Britain's industrial profile lay in the capital goods sector, recognised historically and globally as the headline element of Britain's Industrial Revolution and engineering legacy. This had been accompanied by major decreases in investment in research and development, the consequences of which were highlighted in a series of reports commissioned by the Department of Scientific and Industrial Research in the 1960s.[2] Their author, Geoffrey Feilden, a highly distinguished engineer, made two major observations: first, that the importance of industrial design in an engineering context was widely underestimated by British manufacturers; second, that the engineering profession in Britain was widely considered to have a lower social and economic status than in other highly industrialised competitor countries, and was thus unappealing as a career choice. Furthermore, a 1968 report chaired by Hugh Conway for the Council of Engineering Institutions (CEI) examined the concept of establishing a 'National Council'[3] to embrace the activities, infrastructure and responsibilities of the existing Council of Industrial Design and, additionally, enhance its scope with the introduction of high-level expertise in engineering design. After some prevarication, the government decided to support a refocused and enhanced new body from April 1972, calling it the Design Council. Paul Reilly, director of the Council since 1960, remained in his role at the revamped organisation, bringing his industrial design intelligence and experience to the new larger body – insight that was matched by a formidable injection of engineering knowledge and capability, including that of Feilden and Conway. Feilden became chairman of the new Engineering Design Advisory Committee of the Design Council, and Conway deputy chairman of the Design Council itself.

Even in the early 1970s, many British manufacturers in major industrial centres such as Stoke-on-Trent, Manchester, Sheffield and Birmingham were still suspicious – as they had been for decades – of opinions that sought to persuade them to 'improve' and 'modernise' the design of goods for the home and export markets. This was something of a 'culture war' of the times, since it was not simply a general rejection of a contemporary aesthetic to which captains of industry showed such widespread antipathy. Many of them also lacked enthusiasm for employing graduate artists and designers, often dismissing such applicants as 'arty' individuals, inappropriately dressed and lacking appropriate training or understanding of the demands of industry in the production of profitable design. The true extent to which such attitudes were deeply ingrained in a range of contemporary scenarios has been highlighted in recent research.[4] Ironically, in many cases graduates from art and design schools did not warm to the idea of careers in the manufacturing industry. Lord Esher, Rector of the Royal College of Art, remarked in 1974: 'Industry has only itself to blame. It has not been able to produce an environment where designers are given proper status. Industry must employ designers at a proper level.'[5]

Considerable confusion remained about the design requirements of British manufacturers facing market pressures. Many industrialists were living in a world that no

ABOVE Saatchi & Saatchi, 'Labour isn't working' billboard, 1978. A defining moment in political advertising, this campaign for the Conservative Party used bold, provocative imagery to criticise unemployment under Labour, contributing to Margaret Thatcher's victory in the 1979 general election

longer existed, one in which the belief persisted that overseas consumer markets were clamouring 'for traditional patterns and reproductions of past successes'[6] rather than for goods that favoured the essentially modernist design vocabulary promoted by the Council and professional design bodies such as the Society of Industrial Artists and Designers (SIAD),[7] the International Council of Societies of Industrial Design (ICSID)[8] and the International Council of Graphic Design Associations (ICOGRADA).[9] This latter trio were all concerned with elevating the status of designers, developing ethical codes of professional practice and advocating for the greater benefits that design could offer in a wide range of social, economic and cultural contexts – nationally and globally.

Design consultancies and advertising agencies

After World War II, the growth of British design consultancies was considerable, having been limited in number and size when war broke out in 1939. Prominent British design consultancies in the 1970s included the long-standing Design Research Unit (DRU, established in 1942), by then one of the most widely recognised design agencies in Europe; the corporate identity specialists Wolff Olins (established in 1965), whose early brand successes included Bovis Construction (1971); Michael Peters and Partners (established in 1970), which was known for innovation in the packaging of consumer goods, such as paint packaging and boxes for Winsor & Newton (1973); and the multidisciplinary Pentagram consultancy (established in 1972),[10] with early notable commissions including Kenneth Grange's cab redesign and livery for the Inter-City 125 (or High Speed Train) for British Rail that went into service in 1976. Britain was home, too, to leading advertising agencies including the powerful Boase Massimi Pollitt consultancy (BMP, established in 1968) and Saatchi & Saatchi (established in 1970), which, within a decade, became Britain's largest agency and was widely associated with services for the Conservative Party and Prime Minister Margaret Thatcher. Such agencies developed the technique of account planning,[11] a strategic approach linked to branding and consumer analysis that was seen as an effective business tool. The effectiveness of the levels of design skills and approaches embraced by British multidisciplinary consultancies and advertising agencies had become so attractive to overseas manufacturers and other major business clients that they earned considerable sums by working for foreign clients who were often in direct competition with manufacturers in Britain. A decade later, at the Council's Design Centre in London, this uncomfortable reality provided the basis for the revealing exhibition *Designed in Britain, Made Abroad* (September 1981).

Design on the high street

During the 1970s, many retail outlets and supermarkets encountered in town and city centres across Britain looked to design expertise to enhance their stores, products and presence. Some, like Marks and Spencer, used external design consultants for many of their services, while others, including Sainsbury's supermarkets, appointed in-house design teams. The Sainsbury's design team (established in 1963), led by Peter Dixon, was responsible for the company's striking own-label packaging and information design

Bovis

ABOVE Wolff Olins, logo for house-building firm Bovis, 1971

RIGHT Michael Peters and Partners, Winsor & Newton paint packaging and boxes, 1973. D&AD Silver Award winner

RIGHT   Barbara Hulanicki, Animal print suit, 1972. Synthetic fibre, designed for Biba
BELOW   Habitat, catalogue, 1971

in the 1970s, developed to create an ordered and pleasant shopping experience. Also recognised for affordable yet good-quality design was the Lighting Department at BHS (British Home Stores) led by Roland Millet. By the mid-1970s, it had captured twenty-five per cent of the British market and, despite the import of a small number of stylish designs from Italy and Denmark, the bulk of lighting sales were the outcome of close collaboration between the company's buyers and British manufacturers, and a clear demonstration that there *was* a significant desire for well-designed products in Britain. Britain in the 1970s also saw a proliferation of small design companies and consultancies, who often worked in the lucrative contracts market, designing in fields such as electronics, office equipment, domestic appliances, lighting, kitchenware and textiles. Sisters Susan Collier and Sarah Campbell demonstrated the way in which designers could weave a path from being employed by another company, as they were by Liberty & Co. (1968–77), to working for their own company (established in 1978), through which they designed for a wide range of clients across Britain, including Habitat, Marks and Spencer, Heal's, Jaeger and Liberty, as well as overseas.

Designer–entrepreneur Terence Conran, founder of the Conran Design Group (1956), was quick to realise the potential marketplace for contemporary design in Britain, opening his first Habitat shop in London's Fulham Road in 1964. Aiming to attract a predominantly upwardly mobile, educated and young adult clientele, Habitat responded to customers' growing awareness of different lifestyles and culinary experiences brought about by the considerable growth of travel to the Mediterranean and elsewhere. Habitat customers could select furniture designed by Italian Vico Magistretti, Italian-born American Harry Bertoia, or Britons Rodney Kinsman (OMK Design) and Robin Day. They could furnish their apartments and houses with colourful textiles, such as those by Collier and Campbell, alongside utilitarian, colourful and traditional enamel coffee pots and mugs imported from Poland, or kilims inspired by North Africa and the Middle East. There were numerous goods designed by Conran Associates, too, including the highly popular range of colourful plastic containers manufactured by Crayonne Ltd. Habitat expanded massively during the 1970s, with eighty outlets nationwide by the end of the decade, including a drive-in warehouse with a café and play area in Wythenshawe (1977). It issued its first mail-order catalogue in 1969, with a rapidly growing print run that rose from 300,000 to 1.4 million by 1980, reflecting the company's penetration of overseas markets. It also received a Royal Society for the Encouragement of Arts, Manufactures and Commerce Design Management Award in 1975, at a moment when design management was gaining considerable traction across the design industry.

Several people, including Conran himself at that time, drew comparisons between Habitat and Barbara Hulanicki's Biba (established in 1964, the same year as the first Habitat shop), seeing the former as the furniture equivalent of the latter. While this is debatable, Biba continued to capture the attention of young fashion-conscious consumers with the launch of the Biba cosmetic range in 1970, and moved into its High Street Kensington location in the glamorous

LEFT　　Conran Associates, Input containers, 1973. Design Council Award winner for Crayonne Ltd

BELOW　Kenneth Grange, Inter-City High Speed Train cab redesign and livery for British Rail, 1978. Design Council Award for Engineering Products winner

Art Deco-styled former Derry & Toms department store[12] in 1973, where it remained until Biba's closure in 1975. Biba's High Street Ken shop had opened on the same day as Conran's Habitat store in Kensington.

Transition from Pop to punk

In the wake of Pop art, commentators observed several cultural shifts on the streets of Britain, influenced in part by the increased presence and buying power of college students and young adults, alongside subcultures that embraced challenging modes of behaviour, dress and music. By the 1970s, glam rock's preoccupation with sexuality and gender-typing was evident in the performances, personalities and marketing of David Bowie (Ziggy Stardust), Roxy Music and others. The longer-term impact of Bowie was attested to by the immense popularity of the V&A's 2013 *David Bowie Is* exhibition and the high profile of the David Bowie Centre at V&A East Storehouse, which opens in 2025. Such a seductive outlook contrasted strongly with punk, which also emerged in the 1970s, emanating from what one contemporary researcher described as 'nameless housing estates, anonymous dole queues, slums-in-the-abstract. It was blank, expressionless, rootless.'[13] At the more accessible, yet firmly subversive, edge of this outlook lay the provocations of Vivienne Westwood and Malcolm McLaren, whose King's Road boutique underwent a succession of titles and faces, including SEX (1974), Seditionaries (1977) and World's End (1979). Connected to such assaults on everyday expectations was Jamie Reid, whose graphic work encouraged new typographic possibilities, attracting media outrage with his iconoclastic record sleeve for the Sex Pistols' album *God Save the Queen* (1977). Associated with Westwood as a designer for Seditionaries was Ben Kelly, alumnus of Lancaster College of Art and the RCA, who became influential in shaping Manchester's cultural identity through interiors, record covers and exhibitions. One authority on 'street style' saw all these stimuli as core ingredients in the revitalisation of British fashion, which was on its way to becoming Britain's fourth largest industry.[14]

Design education and emerging ecological and environmental concerns

Art and design education in the 1970s was affected significantly by the recommendations of the NACAE (National Advisory Committee on Art Education, 1958–71) that was chaired by Sir William Coldstream, and the NCDAD (National Council for Diplomas in Art and Design, 1960–74), chaired by Sir John Summerson. Their agenda for change was not an entirely smooth process, especially in 1968 when a series of student sit-ins and occupations of art colleges occurred in Hornsey, Brighton, Guildford, Croydon and other places. In addition, the formation of thirty new polytechnics between 1969 and 1973,[15] a process in which art and design schools were combined with colleges of technology and education to form 'university equivalent' institutions with a vocational edge, resulted in further controversy – including considerable unrest among many lecturers, particularly in the fine arts, who felt that the 'fit' between art and design schools and their new partners would constrain creativity.

Despite the prospect of earning enhanced salaries from employment in industry, many design students (other than entering the teaching profession) were turning towards the establishment of individual studios, small workshops and galleries, often in rural locations. This anti-industrial outlook was a response to a growing interest in environmental and ecological concerns,[16] with many design students rejecting notions of industry and obsolescence, sustained by books such as E. F. Schumacher's *Small is Beautiful* (1973)[17] and Victor Papanek's highly accessible *Design for the Real World: Human Ecology and Social Change*, first published in Britain in 1972.[18] This period of change was also punctuated by national and international meetings that put environmental issues into the foreground, including the landmark 1972 United Nations 'Conference on the Human Environment' in Stockholm, and the 1976 ICSID conference on 'Design for Need' held at the RCA, which sought to address the ethical and moral role of designers in a world of high levels of global consumption and unsustainable levels of mass production. Although the impact of 'green' design was not fully felt until the following decade, awareness of such concerns was consistent and accompanied by a growth of interest in the crafts, which were taught in many art and design schools and polytechnics.

Looking back to the formation of the Design Council in 1972, discussed in the opening paragraph of this chapter, one very important but often overlooked outcome of this marriage between industrial and engineering design was the liberation of the crafts. The Council had experienced a close, but not always comfortable, relationship with the crafts,[19] a relationship dating back to the late 1940s. The Crafts Centre of Great Britain had been established in 1948, supported by a modest grant from the Board of Trade, which also funded the Council, and it was agreed that the latter would have oversight of the Centre on the understanding that the crafts were viewed as an important vehicle for improving standards of industrial design.[20] More than twenty years later, the Crafts Advisory Committee (CAC) was established in 1971 by Lord Eccles, the paymaster general. It was originally under the control of the Council (1971–73), but with a redefining shift of financial support away from the Department of Trade and Industry[21] to the arts branch of the Department of Education and Science (DES). This marked a highly significant change of status, as well as sustainable financial independence, thus enabling a complete break away from the constraints of being tied to the 'creative needs of industry' as the Crafts Centre of Great Britain had been. This sea change sanctioned the role of the *artist*–craftsman as a more experimental individual, freed from considerations of utility – a raison d'être of the designer–craftsman. Just as the new Design Council began to publish *Engineering* magazine, so the CAC announced its new status through publication of *Crafts* in 1973. The CAC moved into new premises just a short walk from the Design Council's Design Centre in Haymarket, and was able to establish a platform for creative and experimental work in many fields, including furniture, ceramics, jewellery, metalware, plastics, weaving and textiles. These works grew increasingly anti-functional and adventurous as the 1970s unfolded, and many exciting new makers came to prominence including ceramicists Alison Britton, Carol McNicoll and Richard Slee; furniture maker Fred Baier; and jewellers Wendy Ramshaw and Stephen Rotholz. Such creators in turn went on to invigorate many design fields in the 1980s.

1. Thomas Weston, 'The UK economy in the 1970s', House of Lords Library (4 April 2024), https://lordslibrary.parliament.uk/the-uk-economy-in-the-1970s/#fn-6, accessed 20 July 2024.
2. Feilden Reports, including *Engineering Design* (1963) and *Industrial Engineering Design* (1965) for the Department of Scientific and Industrial Research.
3. Council of Engineering Design Institutions, *A National Design Council* (the Conway Report) (CEI, 1968).
4. This was well considered by Leah Armstrong in her PhD thesis 'Designing a Profession: The Structure, Organisation and Identity of the Design Profession in Britain 1930–2010' (University of Brighton, 2014). Her recent book *The Industrialised Designer: Gender, Identity and Professionalization in Britain and the United States* (Manchester: Manchester University Press, 2024) addresses such issues directly and in detail.
5. Leader, *Design* (January 1974), 301.
6. 'Commercial Exploitation', *CoID: Twenty-fourth Annual Report 1968–1969* (London: HMSO, 1969), 4–5.
7. Formed as the Society of Industrial Artists (SIA) in 1930 and becoming, in 1987, the Chartered Society of Designers (CSD).
8. Founded in 1957; since 2017, the World Design Organization.
9. Founded in 1963; since 2013, the International Council of Design.
10. Peter Gorb, *Living by Design: Partners of Pentagram* (London: Lund Humphries, 1978).
11. The Account Planners Group was established in 1978.
12. Designed by Bernard George in 1933, with metalwork by Walter Gilbert and a rooftop garden by Ralph Hancock.
13. Dick Hebdige, *Subculture: The Meaning of Style* (London: Methuen, 1979), 63.
14. Catherine McDermott, *Street Style: British Design in the 80s* (London: Design Council, 1987), 24.
15. This was in response to the *Robbins Report on Higher Education*, chaired by Lord Robbins (HMSO, 1963).
16. This has been usefully covered in a pioneering article: Pauline Madge, 'Design, Ecology, Technology: A Historiographic Review', *Journal of Design History* 6/3 (1993), 14ff.
17. E. F. Schumacher, *Small is Beautiful: a study of economics as if people mattered* (London: Blond & Briggs, 1973).
18. Victor Papanek, *Design for the Real Word: Human Ecology and Social Change* (London: Thames & Hudson, 1972). First published in the United States in 1971.
19. See Tanya Harrod, *Crafts in Britain in the 20th Century* (London: BARD/Yale University Press, 1999), especially Chapter 10.
20. James Noel White, 'The First Crafts Centre of Great Britain: Bargaining for a Time Bomb', *Journal of Design History* 2/2–3, 207–14.
21. Formerly the Board of Trade and Industry and a major funder of the Design Council.

ABOVE   Lancer Boss, 3500 and 2500 series container-handling sideloaders, 1972. Design Council Capital Goods Award Winner
OPPOSITE   Malcolm McLaren and Vivienne Westwood, 'Destroy' muslin shirt, 1978. Designed for Seditionaries, Kings Road, Chelsea

ABOVE Carol McNicoll, *Untitled (Ceramics & Glass)*, 1973
RIGHT Fred Baier, Stained Sycamore Upright Chair, 1978
OPPOSITE Freddie Burretti, Ziggy Stardust tour suit, 1972. Quilted two-piece worn by David Bowie on 'Top of the Pops'

OPPOSITE Trellis Paisley, 1968

Trellis Paisley
A Heritage Motif Reborn

Dating back to 1968, Trellis Paisley was designed as a border for a Liberty scarf. This print features delicate, paisley-inspired flowers that emerge from a series of filled *boteh* (Persian bush or bud) shapes, creating an organic ornamental canopy. Framed by a sharp diagonal check, this statement pattern creates a bold visual juxtaposition of clashing styles and colours.

Originating in ancient Persia and India, the iconic paisley motif carries layers of hidden meanings and mysterious symbolism. In 1875, exquisite Kashmir textiles and intricate paisleys graced the shawl department of the Liberty emporium in London, cementing a lasting connection with the brand. The 1970s saw Liberty paisleys take centre stage once more, embraced by rock stars and celebrities with a penchant for flamboyant, expressive fashion. Reinvented with a modern edge, these timeless patterns became vibrant and daring, enriched by a bohemian spirit and often paired with stripes, checks or geometric motifs. This diverse design genre bridged Eastern and Western influences, attracting a following among the progressive and rebellious.

The 1980s

Design and Commerce

Shifting Horizons: The Design Council in a New Economy
Lesley Whitworth

The 1980s opened in recession, with an administration committed to restraining public expenditure. The real-time effect of 1970s inflation was now deepened by a ten per cent cut to the Design Council's grant-in-aid for 1981–2, repeated in 1985–6, with predictable impacts on staff numbers.[1] Conversely, this was also the decade of the Downing Street Design seminars, and the UK-wide 'Design for Profit' seminar series spearheaded by John Butcher MP, Parliamentary Under Secretary of State for Industry.[2]

In the regions, twenty-four officers based at offices in London, Glasgow, Cardiff, Wolverhampton, Belfast and later Manchester[3] continued to help 500 companies stay current as part of the Design Advisory Service (DAS), increasingly navigating complex modern technology when few companies understood the potential of microprocessors. Importantly, the scheme brought about a significant expansion of Britain's design ecosystem by generating contracts for independent design advice.[4] Despite this, in 1983 Britain exported fewer manufactured goods than it imported for the first time since the Industrial Revolution.[5] Upsettingly, some of these foreign products were now designed by Britons, as the Council's own exhibitions in 1981 and 1988 illustrated.[6]

As the decade opened, Design Index acceptances were running at forty per cent, arguably because of greater stringency, and in 1982 there were 7,000 products in the renamed Design Centre Selection.[7] However, this hid the fact that more labels were being bought by fewer manufacturers, prompting the launch of a redesigned label in 1985.

Piecemeal refurbishment of the Design Centre continued. In the early '80s, the enlarged shop offered 5,000 products from 250 manufacturers. Turnover rose by forty-five per cent and café sales doubled.[8] The buzz of 1980s fashion and design was very evident.[9] Design Centre Selection moved to a lower floor, where it continued expanding its categories: motor vehicles, building products, products for people with disabilities, and footwear. A new Data Protection Service offered advice where the threat of plagiarism arose.[10] The Innovation Centre that opened in 1985 was a notable addition, made possible by an annually changing

PREVIOUS PAGE Cesar Pelli with Adamson Associates and Frederick Gibberd Coombes, One Canada Square, 1981-91. This iconic fifty-storey skyscraper in Canary Wharf became London's tallest building upon completion and symbolised the transformation of London's Docklands into a major financial district

ABOVE *Designed in Britain, Made Abroad* poster for exhibition at the Design Centre, 1981

roster of sponsors. The booklet accompanying its launch was in demand from university and college lecturers in design management.[11]

The viewing public continued to visit. In five weeks, 113,000 saw the *Miles Ahead* exhibition about car design, now an important sector for the Council, and, reviving an old format, 100,000 visited a show house in Milton Keynes in January 1981. Exhibitions included *Design & Disability* and *Design for Need*, marking the twenty-fifth anniversary of the Intermediate Technology Group, which had a social dimension; and *Design for Profit* and *Design and the Economy*, with blunter imperatives. Three exhibitions revealed design's past instead of its more typical future: a Gordon Russell retrospective,[12] *SIAD: Fifty Years of British Design*[13] and *30 Years On*, a Design Centre retrospective. The annual tally of visitors from 1985–86 was 929,830.[14] The Council began utilising venues in addition to its own, including in Aberdeen, Barnsley, Swansea, Manchester and Edinburgh. From 1983, dedicated funding also made it possible to transfer Council exhibitions to Northern Ireland. The Council was represented at the usual round of trade fairs and, in a rapprochement with the British Council and Central Office of Information, Design Council staff helped create *Designers in Britain*, which toured South America.

From mid-1982, the Council administered a Department of Industry scheme that eclipsed its DAS offer. It made fifteen hours of free design consultancy available to medium-sized businesses (60–1,000 employees), with fifteen more part-subsidised hours possible. Three years' allocation was committed within twelve months, and then raised to £10 million. Although nearly £800,000-worth of consultancy was still facilitated by DAS outside this Funded Consultancy Scheme,[15] rising to £1.5 million in 1986–87,[16] it necessarily dominated the work of the regional offices.[17] Subsequent tranches were accompanied by a reorientation to small firms (1–500 employees), resulting in a seventy per cent increase in Welsh applications. Small firms were an identifiable theme. A *Small Firms, Big Ideas* exhibition brought useful attention to start-ups and entrepreneurial endeavour, and the Mobil Design Award for small firms was inaugurated with a prize of £10,000 and marketing advice.

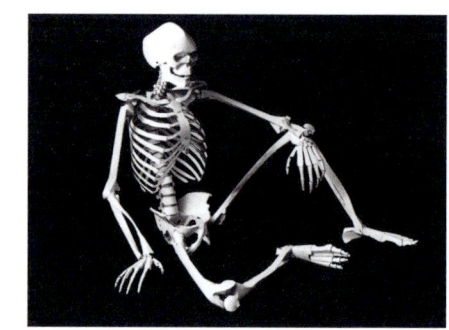

ABOVE   Richard Miller, Fisher-Miller Human Skeleton, 1986. The award-winning Fisher-Miller self-assembly card skeleton was a fully articulated, anatomically correct teaching aid

BELOW   The label design for the Design Centre Selection was refreshed in 1985 (left); Poster from the 1980s promoting the Design Centre's enhanced retail offer (right)

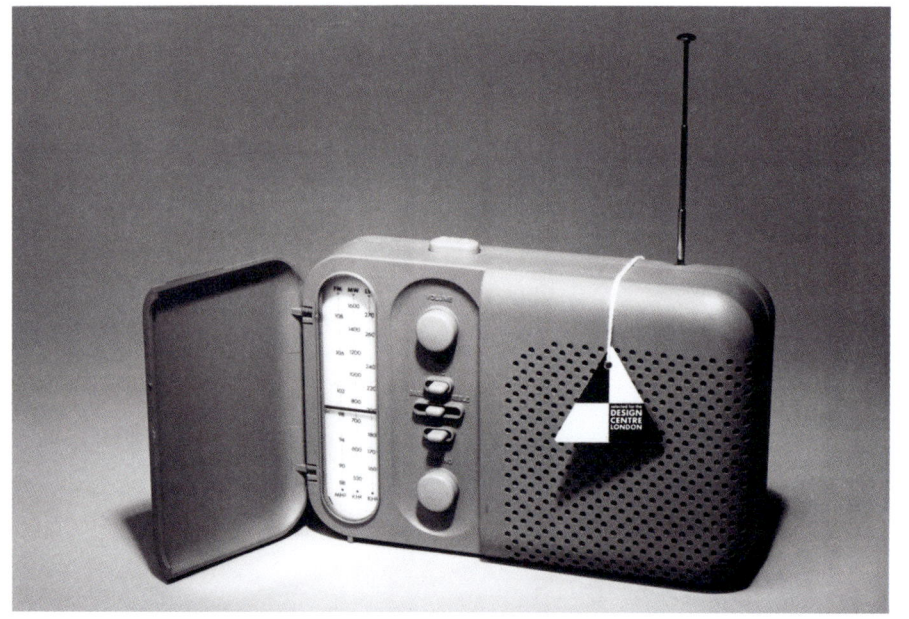

RIGHT   Rolls-Royce Wide-Chord Fan Blade, 1985

BELOW   Adrian Espin, Lawrence Rao and Roger Wareham, Easy PC Program, 1989. Made by Number One Systems Ltd, this program was an award winner in the Computer Software category from 1989

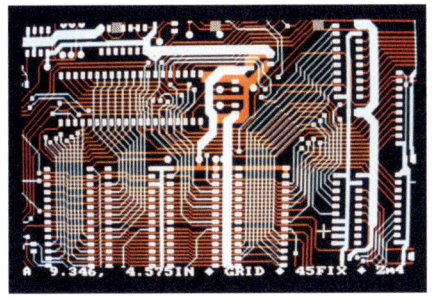

ABOVE   Louisa Slater, Spirals, 1988. A jewellery range laser-cut from Formica Colorcore and winner of a British Design Award

Progress in the country's constituent parts was uneven – all had distinct activities. In Wales, which had no degree-level course in industrial design and where an acute problem with product development existed, the need for better-located Council premises with seminar and exhibition facilities could not be met.[18] For so long the beneficiary of discrete funding and a well-appointed Design Centre,[19] Scotland lost its independent Scottish Committee in 1982 when stronger Scottish representation on the main Council was proposed instead.[20] The Council did not distinguish itself in Belfast, where one of its most visible activities was a competition called 'Opportunity Ulster', promoted on Ulster TV and shown at the Ulster Museum. Indicative of the times, its *Investment in Design* exhibition was bombed.

Meanwhile, the Council's publishing arm maintained strong results, including a successful design history series.[21] *Engineering* magazine continued to win plaudits, and the scope of *Design* magazine was now described as 'broad developments in industrial, interior and graphic design'. Both journals carried articles reflecting the government's 'Year of IT' in 1982. Interestingly, there was no book equivalent to the *Green Designer* exhibition of 1986 until Paul Burall's *Green Design* in 1991.[22]

The most significant expansion of the Council's offerings at this time was educational. The final report of a Design Council working party chaired by Professor David Keith-Lucas marked a significant intervention in the education landscape when it arrived in September 1980, proposing a national policy for design education at secondary level. Next steps entailed promoting A-level Design for university entrance; more and better trained design teachers; and a national body for school-based design education embracing craft, design and technology, and art and design, as well as home economics. This last proved difficult, prompting Council director Keith Grant to chair a forum instead. The Engineering Professors' Conference gave its approval to A-level design qualifications and the UK's examination boards produced models that met the Keith-Lucas criteria. In a long-awaited corollary, the Engineering Council

ABOVE   Poster for the Molins Design Prize, 1985. One of many co-sponsored prizes administered by the Design Council, it is aimed at students of engineering and engineering science

OPPOSITE   *Small Firms: Big Ideas* exhibition poster, 1980

made a design component mandatory in the teaching of graduates seeking chartered engineer status.[23]

Supported by multiple partners,[24] the Council launched *DESIGNING*, a thrice-yearly schools' newspaper that achieved 6,000 paid subscriptions by 1984, meaning 30,000 teachers and ten times as many students were reading each issue.[25] It proposed to the Secretary of State for Trade and Industry that it should consequently consider design-related education at primary level. The Council duly reported after visiting eighty schools and gathering evidence from expert witnesses.[26] To continue the discussion, it launched *The Big Paper* in September 1987 with a flurry of seminars, and by 1988 around half of Britain's 25,000 primary schools were taking it.[27] It launched *Engineering Design Education*, too, a twice-yearly paper for teachers on engineering, technical and functional design courses. Alongside this, it administered the ongoing Schools Design Prize; disbursed Department of Industry funds for work on curriculum development; and considered teaching resources, including producing its own slide and video series with accompanying booklets. Naturally, when the government began working out the details of its proposed National Curriculum, the Council could make well-honed submissions about design.

Against such solid progress – and with the popular success of the BBC Design Awards, with which it was associated, still resonant – the findings of a commissioned report into future strategy could not have been foreseen.[28] This devastating precursor to the 1994 Sorrell Review led to the cessation of trade-fair exhibitions, design selection and retailing. The Council would continue administering the design elements of the Department of Trade and Industry's 'Enterprise Initiative', which was felt to have superseded its own Design Advisory Service. Its expertise in managing around £1 million-worth of awards programming for itself and others was acknowledged as a core competency, earning it £200,000 in fees.[29] 'The Council will,' it wrote, 'continually be looking for new areas where its role can be developed.'[30]

1 By 1981, there were fifteen per cent fewer staff than three years previously. Design Council, *Annual Report, 1980–81*, 6.
2 John Butcher MP is well represented in the Design Council's photographic record and was the recipient in 1986 of the Royal Society for the Encouragement of Arts, Manufactures and Commerce (RSA) Bicentenary Medal for contributing to the improvement of industrial design.
3 The latter premises were at Waterloo Road, Wolverhampton; Piccadilly Plaza, Manchester; and Windsor House, Bedford Street, Belfast.
4 The 1984 edition of the *Directory of Design Expertise* contained twice as many entries as its predecessor. Design Council, *Annual Report, 1983–84*, 15.
5 Kerry Schott, 'Economic Competitiveness and Design', *Journal of the Royal Society of Arts* 132/5,338 (1984), 648–59.
6 The exhibitions were *Designed in Britain, Made Abroad* (1981) and *Drawn from Britain* (1988).
7 Design Council, *Annual Report, 1979–80*, 7, and *Annual Report 1981–82*, 8.
8 Design Council, *Annual Report, 1981–82*, 9.
9 See Catherine McDermott, *Street Style: British Design in the 80s* (London: Design Council, 1987).
10 Design Council, *Annual Report, 1986–87*, 10.
11 The booklet was written by the Science Policy Research Unit of the University of Sussex.
12 Sir Gordon Russell CBE, MC, died in October 1980. The Gordon Russell Furniture Award was launched in 1984.
13 Society of Industrial Artists and Designers, now the Chartered Society of Designers.
14 Design Council, *Annual Report, 1985–86*, 22.
15 'Support for Design' from 1 April 1985.
16 This rose to £1.5 million in consultants' fees generated by a DAS membership of 1,114 in 1986–87. Design Council, *Annual Report, 1986–87*, 8.
17 Design Council, *Annual Report, 1984–85*, 5.
18 An event targeted at 'Getting the Product Right' was held elsewhere in Cardiff in October 1980.
19 The Scottish Design Centre also benefited from major reconstruction work in spring 1984, when it gained improved exhibition space, an upgraded retail offer and a café.
20 Design Council, *Annual Report, 1981–82*, 11.
21 ibid., 10.
22 On the complicated trajectory of environmental concerns, see Pauline Madge, 'Ecological Design: A New Critique', *Design* 13/2 (1997), 44–54.
23 The problem, however, did not resolve itself easily. See D. F. Sheldon, 'How to Teach Engineering and Industrial Design: A UK Experience', *European Journal of Engineering Education* 13/2 (1988), 103–15.
24 The initial sponsors were the Department of Industry; the Department of Education and Science; BP International Ltd; the Orlando Oldham Charitable Trust; the RSA; and, later, the Crafts Council.
25 Design Council, *Annual Report, 1986–87*, 15.
26 Design Council, *Annual Report, 1983–84*, 10, and *Annual Report, 1986–87*, 12.
27 Design Council, *Annual Report, 1981–82*, 10, and *Annual Report, 1983–84*, 15.
28 The 'Design Council Strategy Development Report' (1988) was commissioned from SRU Ltd by the Design Council. For context, see Jonathan M. Woodham, 'Design and the State: Post-War Horizons and Pre-Millennial Aspirations', in D. J. Huppatz (ed.), *Design: Critical and Primary Sources – Vol.4: Development, Globalization, Sustainability* (London and New York: Bloomsbury, 2016), 99–114.
29 Design Council, *Design Review 1988* (1988), 12.
30 Ibid., 20.

The Design Decade: The Big Bang and its Aftermath
Deyan Sudjic

The 1980s are far enough removed from our present day-to-day traumas to have taken on the air of a comfortable costume drama. Enormous mobile phones and shoulder pads have become harmless period-establishing signifiers, much as Mary Quant and Biba outfits are used to represent the preceding decades. They allow us to look back on the '80s as if the period were some kind of *Downton Abbey* streaming series, safely lost in nostalgic detail. Look, isn't that a Mark III Ford Escort? Did Katharine Hamnett really wear that '58% Don't Want Pershing' T-shirt to Downing Street?

In reality, the decade was anything but comfortable – it saw a violent transformation of Britain. Entire manufacturing categories were shut down and, whether it liked it or not, the country was being forcibly converted into a service economy. For bankers and brokers and perhaps some designers, this was an attractive prospect. The Big Bang deregulation of financial services turned London into a centre for footloose capital second only to Manhattan. It made possible the building of Canary Wharf, Europe's second largest financial centre after the City of London itself, rescuing eight square miles of crumbling dockland from dereliction. In 1988, when construction started on its centrepiece, Cesar Pelli's stainless-steel-skinned tower One Canada Square, the tallest skyscraper in Britain at the time, King Charles was still the Prince of Wales. Fresh from his triumph in torpedoing a Mies van der Rohe design for a svelte bronze glass tower at Mansion House, he asked Pelli, 'Why does it have to be so tall?' Pelli was too polite to tell him that Canary Wharf needed a signpost visible from the Square Mile if it was going to attract tenants. At the other end of London, bankers bonuses transformed Notting Hill from edgy bohemia to frozen affluence.

For the 300,000 miners and the 100,000 steel workers thrown out of work over the course of the decade, the prosperity of the South East was little consolation. In 1983, three million days were lost to strikes – many of them in the fight against redundancies. Unemployment passed the three-million mark and inflation reached twenty-two per cent. Amid this upheaval, one constant loomed large: Margaret Thatcher. Having defeated Labour's James Callaghan to take power in 1979, she remained in office until 1990. She survived an IRA bomb planted in the Brighton hotel in which she was preparing her speech for the Conservative Party Conference; riots that left Handsworth, Tottenham, Brixton and Moss Side burning; a year-long miners' strike that resembled a medieval battle between police and trade unions; and a war with Argentina.

Thatcher used her term in office to bring Britain's post-war political consensus to an abrupt end. Council house-building policies pursued by both main parties came to an almost complete halt. She demonised social housing and sold 1.5 million council homes at a steep discount to their market value to turn Britain into a nation of property owners. Moreover, starting with telephones, public utilities including water, gas and electricity were privatised. Repackaging state-owned enterprises for privatisation would indeed become a useful source of work for a select group of design consultancies.

British Telecom was hived off from the GPO, as the Post Office used to be known, and then sold on in 1984. The job of transforming it from an essential utility into an asset

ABOVE Richard Rogers, The Lloyd's building, London, 1985

class was handled by two very un-1980s designers. Colin Banks and John Miles were typographers, technically adept in the world of metal type. They belonged to a generation still rooted in the belief that design had a social mission – the 'herbivores', as Hugh Casson had once described the designers who took part in the 1951 Festival of Britain.

Banks and Miles's previous clients included the Consumers' Association and the Greater London Council. They had modernised the GPO with a pillar-box-red identity, a convincing new font and a fresh look for the Royal Crown. For BT, they took off the Crown, which was clearly not going to be for sale, and replaced it with a simplistic new logo involving a T in a circle, a lurid blue-and-yellow colour scheme, and dot-and-dash metaphors for digital communication.

Unlike other privatisations, such as the fiasco of the water companies, there were certain advantages for BT in joining the market. It no longer took a three-month wait for a new landline to be installed, for instance, and the telephone itself turned into a consumer item rather than a piece of government property that you were allowed to rent but not own. But there was something about Banks and Miles's new look for BT that did not quite gel with the privatisation zeitgeist, and it was quickly abandoned in favour of the so-called 'Prancing Piper' branding devised by Wolff Olins.

The lesson that it was necessary to find a designer with the right commercial instincts had been learned by the time that British Airways set out on the same privatisation path in 1984. Rather than risking another herbivorous British designer triggering a misfire, BA brought in the slick American branding firm of Landor to do the job. Landor painted

BELOW   Landor Associates, identity for British Airways, 1984 (top); Newell and Sorrell, identity for British Airways, 1997 (bottom)

OPPOSITE   Paul Smith in his Covent Garden shop, 1984. Known for blending classic tailoring with playful touches, Smith's shop also featured an eclectic mix of products, including clocks, calculators and stationery, reflecting his unique retail approach

LEFT   Colin Banks and John Miles, identity for BT, 1981 (top); Wolff Olins, BT Piper logo on which Peter Denmark worked as illustrator, 1991 (bottom)

a so-called laser-flash red stripe along the side of the hull of BA's aircraft, and added a simplified coarsened crest to the tail, a combination that looked worryingly close to what they had put on the front of a cigarette packet that they had recently designed for an American client. Margaret Thatcher liked it so much that, years later, she was photographed at the British Airways booth at the Conservative Party Conference wrapping her handkerchief around the tail plane of a model aircraft decorated in Newell and Sorrell's Union Jack-free, so-called 'ethnic' livery, which briefly replaced Landor's branding, in disgust.

Next in line for privatisation were the industries in which the government had a stake. British Airways was followed by Rolls-Royce and the state-owned car builder British Leyland (BL). BL had once employed more than 150,000 people and had the capacity to make more than a million cars a year. Unfortunately, nobody wanted to buy the Triumph Acclaim, the Austin Montego or the Morris Marina. After the sale, none of the new owners prospered and most of the brands vanished. If there was a British carmaker working effectively with design, it was Colin Chapman, who launched the Lotus Esprit Turbo in 1980 before his sudden death in 1982 in the midst of a legal investigation into his role in the DeLorean scandal.

While manufacturing was in steep decline, there were signs of new life in what would come to be known as the creative industries. British fashion designers Paul Smith and Margaret Howell were just starting out as the decade began. Joseph Ettedgui commissioned Eva Jiricna to design his clothing shops. Sheridan Coakley set up the furniture company SCP with designs by Jasper Morrison, Konstantin Grcic and Matthew Hilton. Neville Brody created a distinctive look for *The Face* magazine. Ben Kelly designed the Haçienda club in Manchester, while Peter Saville did album covers for New Order.

In 1986, James Dyson began selling the G-Force bagless vacuum cleaner – coloured a 'sex-toy' shade of pink – in Japan, leading to the product that put him among Britain's handful of industrial billionaires. Other design-conscious industrial UK contenders from the period did less well. Clive Sinclair, for example, who made a brilliant start with the ZX personal computers, crashed and burned with the misconceived C5 electric vehicle.

The way that Britain thinks about design has always been self-contradictory. It has been understood as either a cultural or a commercial matter, occasionally both at the same time. For William Morris, it was certainly about moral virtue and about making the world a better place. Raymond Loewy, on the other hand, talked persuasively about streamlining the sales curve. He claimed he had boosted sales of Lucky Strike cigarettes by changing the colour of the pack from green to white. It was the latter version that would have appealed to Margaret Thatcher and which most characterised the 1980s. She could see that design was about repackaging Britain and about making people rich; and she understood at some level that it was the design of Sony televisions and Nissan cars that made British consumers choose them ahead of their British equivalents. She approved a knighthood for Terence Conran, even though he saw himself as an unspecified kind of

ABOVE & OPPOSITE Ben Kelly and Morph, FAC51, The Haçienda, east and west views, 2009. Designed by Ben Kelly and opened in 1982, The Haçienda became one of the most influential nightclubs of its era, pioneering Manchester's acid house movement with its industrial aesthetic, bold graphic identity and repurposed materials before closing in 1997

socialist. She held a seminar on design at Downing Street and maintained government support for the Design Council – although pushing it to focus more on policy than on the public, a direction that would lead to the closure of the popular shop in the Design Centre on Haymarket.

When Conran built the Design Museum in 1989 – in a former banana-ripening warehouse made over to look like the 'Bauhaus on the Thames' – Thatcher agreed to declare it open. But as a patron of design, she hardly matched the example of the French president at the time. François Mitterand was busy commissioning Philippe Starck to design the furniture in his private rooms at the Élysée Palace, as well as building I. M. Pei's Pyramid at the Louvre.

When the world started to pay attention to what was happening to design in Britain, it was not the big commercial firms that were the attraction. Japanese clients looked for radical young talent in London. They found Nigel Coates and David Chipperfield, and hired them to build in Tokyo. Coates designed the Caffè Bongo for the Seibu department store while Chipperfield's career got a kickstart with a commission from Issey Miyake. Without any clients for their work, Ron Arad, Tom Dixon and Jasper Morrison began their careers by making things themselves, a phenomenon that the Crafts Council later celebrated with its *Industry of One* exhibition.

In 1988, the Institute of Contemporary Arts (ICA) brought a selection of this generation together for an exhibition titled *Metropolis*. In addition to Arad and Coates, it included John Pawson and Zaha Hadid. Architecture and design magazine *Blueprint* launched in 1983 with a party on the construction site of Richard Rogers' Lloyd's building, another skyscraper that came to define the decade.

The postmodern wave sweeping the worlds of design and architecture in the 1980s was laced with a strong dose of celebrity. For about five minutes in 1984, the most fashionable bar on the most fashionable street in Paris was called the Café Costes. It was not the food or the wine list that packed them in: it was the chance to spend half an hour sitting on a three-legged chair in Philippe Starck's very first interior, waiting for a coffee that never came. Café Costes triggered the plague of celebrity-focused designer kettles, designer hotels, designer mineral water, designer pasta, designer toothbrushes and all the other useless paraphernalia of the time. In Milan, Ettore Sottsass and the Memphis Group were undermining the assumptions of modernism in design. Philip Johnson and John Burgee completed the Chippendale-style AT&T tower on Madison Avenue, with its broken-pediment rooftop, in 1984. All of them began to appear as faces on the covers of design magazines.

The 1980s was often called 'the design decade', partly because it was the period in which a certain subset of the design world turned from a cottage industry into a real business with stock-market listings, company cars and account handlers – just like the largest advertising firms. For Michael Peters and Rodney Fitch, the two most prominent examples of this phenomenon, the experiment did not end well. After a brief moment of pomp, which saw them spend heavily on impressive office buildings in London, they both lost control of their businesses. So too did Terence Conran, who injected his design consultancy into the offer when

LEFT Design Museum, Shad Thames, 1989. Founded by Sir Terence Conran, the museum opened in a converted banana warehouse, becoming the UK's first institution dedicated to contemporary design

RIGHT   Neville Brody, *The Face*, Grace Jones on the cover of the January 1986 issue

BELOW   Margaret Howell, Autumn/Winter collection, 1982. Howell reworked classic British menswear for women, offering a relaxed alternative to the bold power dressing of the era

floating Habitat on the stock market in 1981. The initial sale of shares went well, and got the money markets interested in what he could do next. He was given the investment to take over British Home Stores and build Storehouse, a group with a £1 billion turnover. While it turned him from a designer into a tycoon, it did not save him from a boardroom coup when his makeover plan for the British Home Stores did not make sufficiently rapid progress. Although it was a traumatic experience, he did better out of it than either Peters or Fitch, who went back to being employees. Conran was able to retain ownership of the Conran Shop, and to establish a restaurant empire. Peters, however, was given the chance to redraw the Conservative Party symbol: working directly with Thatcher, he added a hand to hold the burning-torch brand that it was using at the time.

Before things turned sour, Conran used some of the money he made from the flotation to start the Design Museum. He began with the Boilerhouse Project, a prototype for the museum housed in the basement of the Victoria and Albert Museum. His intention was to inject a new energy into the V&A, an institution that had been founded by Henry Cole with the profits made by the Great Exhibition of 1851. Cole wanted a forward-looking institution to teach students and advise industry. But after his time, innate British cultural scepticism of commerce reasserted itself and the V&A became a museum of the decorative arts – exquisite, but more about the past than the future. It had, for example, never shown a motor car until 1983, when a Ford was craned into position for an exhibition in the Boilerhouse. It was followed by shows on Issey Miyake and national characteristics in design. The V&A is a very different museum now, but in those days its curators were resistant to change of any kind. After being unimpressed by an exhibition on the branding of Coca-Cola, Conran realised that he could only create his idea of what a design museum should be by doing it himself, and left South Kensington for Docklands.

The first show at the new Design Museum, which opened in 1989, was called *Culture and Commerce*. It was designed by David Davies, responsible for the look of the new chain of Next shops. But overall it was an emblematic summation of the paradoxes of the decade. In an inevitable swing of the pendulum, the earnestness of the 1970s – when Victor Papanek wrote *Design for the Real World*, his blistering attack on the complicity of designers in the disposable wastefulness of consumerism – was seen as hopelessly old hat in the 1980s. Since then, the compensatory swing back has encouraged another generation to ask some of the same questions that Papanek did. In the end, it is the cultural aspects of design that allowed it to survive the 1980s and the part it played in sugar-coating the realities of post-industrialisation.

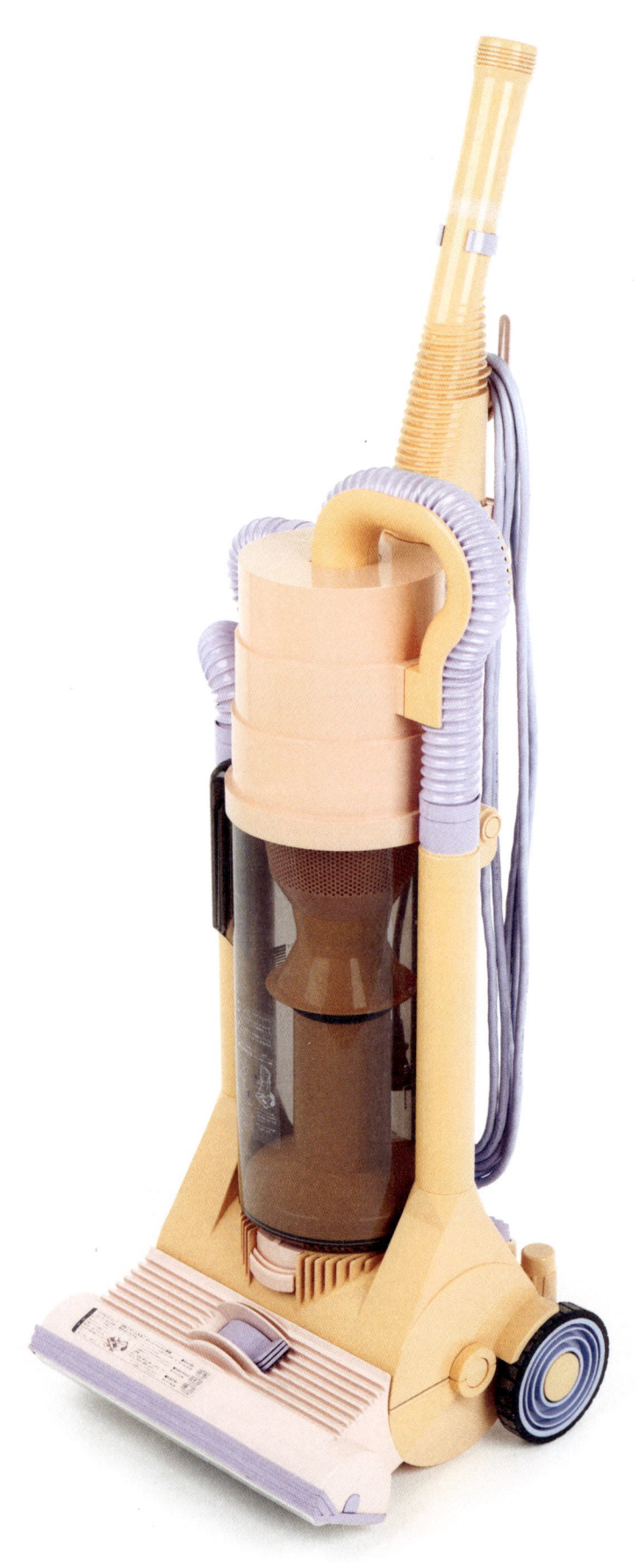

OPPOSITE   James Dyson, G-Force vacuum cleaner, 1983. Designed by Dyson and manufactured by Japanese company APEX in 1986, this early bagless vacuum pioneered cyclonic separation technology

LEFT   John Pawson, display for the *Hand Tools* exhibition, Boilerhouse Project, V&A, 1984. Pawson's minimalist design highlighted the craftsmanship and function of everyday tools, foreshadowing his architectural approach

BELOW   David Chipperfield, Issey Miyake Sloane Street store, London, 1985. Chipperfield's minimalist design reflected Miyake's innovative approach to fashion, using raw materials and clean lines to create a striking, modern retail space

LIBERTY.

OPPOSITE Memphis Leaf, 1982

Memphis Leaf
Bold Geometry and Postmodern Play

Memphis Leaf was created in 1982, as a hand-painted corner of a Liberty scarf. This whimsical geometric design perfectly captures the spirit of the 1980s, showcasing a lively mix of shapes in almost-neon colours. Scattered simplified leaves are framed by symmetrically arranged square borders and accented with polka dots, resulting in an engaging visual interplay.

Stepping into the 1980s in style, Liberty designs embraced the prevailing fashion trends of the period. With a focus on hand-painted geometrics, scarves and dress fabrics were decorated with playful shapes and collaged abstract motifs in clashing colours, giving them a dynamic spontaneity. Inspired by the influential Memphis Milano design movement, these graphic patterns combined unexpected elements in unique ways. Liberty celebrated this avant-garde spirit further in 1983 by hosting an exhibition of the Memphis Group, whose abstract, sculptural forms and clashing optical patterns left a lasting imprint on the era's textiles.

The 1990s

Design for a Connected World

Rebirth and Renewal: The Design Council Under Threat
Jeremy Myerson

The early 1990s were not a happy time for the Design Council. The high profile and the political patronage of the Thatcher years were fast disappearing in the rear-view mirror. Under director Ivor Owen, the Design Council had managed to alienate large sections of the design community with an excessive focus on engineering, and its raison d'être was being threatened by government plans to deliver industrial services, including design advice, through the newly formed Business Link service.

The organisation was widely seen as out of touch and bloated, too, with more than 200 staff, an annual grant of £7.5 million from the Department of Trade and Industry, and an expensive lease on its once-flagship Haymarket House premises. By 1993, relations with the government had deteriorated to the point where there was a serious question mark over its future. The Council faced the chop, its isolation almost terminal. Yet, by the end of the decade, it was again right at the heart of things, fully aligned with Tony Blair's campaign around 'Creative Britain', reconnected to designers of all stripes, and miraculously enjoying political support at the highest levels of government and business.

The story of the Design Council in the 1990s is therefore one of rebirth and renewal in a vibrant new slimline form after a near-death experience. Back in 1993, things could not have been worse. *Financial Times* management editor Christopher Lorenz, himself a member of the Council, wrote in his regular column: 'In retrospect, the Design Council might have been treated more kindly by Whitehall if it had managed to restore the high-profile campaigning image for which it was noted in the 1970s and which the government now wants revised and redirected to the business world.'

Many in the design press saw its demise as inevitable. Deyan Sudjic, design correspondent for *The Guardian* at the time, wryly observed that the Design Council 'has been written off so many times that it is hard to believe that it has finally been despatched'.[1] The reason for such speculation was that in September 1993, Minister for Industry Tim Sainsbury announced a major review of the Council's activities. The task of leading the review was given to John Sorrell, a

PREVIOUS PAGE Alexander McQueen, Ready-to-Wear Spring/Summer 1999 fashion show at London Fashion Week, 27 September 1998. One of McQueen's most iconic presentations, the show featured robotic arms spray-painting model Shalom Harlow's white dress live on stage – a moment that cemented his reputation for theatrical, boundary-pushing design and reinforced Britain's influence on avant-garde fashion

BELOW The Design Council, *Project 2045* exhibition, 1995. This Council event asked people to imagine the world in 2045. The event involved sending time capsules to schools, organisations and individuals. The capsules will be opened fifty years after the exhibition

prominent design consultant, former chairman of the Design Business Association and a leading spokesman for the design community, who had become a member of the Council in January 1992.

Sorrell was convinced that the Design Council should be updated rather than axed. He believed that bridges could be rebuilt with the design community and that the organisation could find a new purpose. Bringing great energy and focus to the review, Sorrell withdrew from running his own successful design business, Newell and Sorrell, to concentrate full-time on getting the Council into better shape.

Between October 1993 and January 1994, Sorrell's review consulted hundreds of organisations right across business, education, research and the public sector. Opinions were sought. Evidence was gathered. What emerged was the blueprint for a new Design Council with a revised purpose, smarter objectives, a clear strategy and an agile structure. This blueprint was described in a report, *The Future Design Council*, which was submitted to the government in early 1994.

The Sorrell Report, as the review document became known colloquially, sketched out a new organisational model that was a radical departure from what had gone before: a small, lean, collaborative body with around forty staff dedicated to disseminating knowledge and catalysing change. The Design Council should have a new purpose: 'To inspire the best use of design by the United Kingdom in the world context, in order to improve prosperity and well-being.'[2] It should advise government and other bodies on design policy. It should itself become an exemplar for the effective use of design. And it should devote more of its budget to design activities and less to fixed overheads like salaries and rent. Critically, it should stop commercial publishing, service delivery and other revenue-generating activities to concentrate on research, education and communication.

The recommendations in the report were accepted by the government in full in March 1994. Sorrell then partnered with a career civil servant, Evelyn Ryle, to make the organisation's transition from the old structure to the new happen.

Later, in January 1995, a new chief executive, Andrew Summers, would be recruited to run the reinvented organisation. Summers had a strong marketing and management background, having worked at a senior level in the international food industry, and the new CEO quickly became a key player in establishing this fresh direction. No more of the 'Director-Generals' from years past – the language around the organisation was changing fast, and the narrative was set to change too.

Sorrell's design experiences in the commercial world coloured the approach. An expert in corporate identity, he understood clearly that the Council's new purpose could only be achieved if its image changed and external perceptions altered. A series of tactical projects were therefore put in place to signal the new strategy and effectively 'relaunch' the Design Council.

The first, Project 2045, invited 2,045 different participants – from captains of industry to primary-school children – to predict what the world would be like in 2045. The results were buried in time capsules to be opened in fifty years' time. A second initiative was a national competition, 'Design Visions', to redesign the Houses of Parliament, whose main debating chamber was widely seen as contributing to the confrontational nature of British politics.

The Design Council's creative credentials were polished further by a move from Haymarket House to a former telephone exchange in London's Covent Garden. Interior designer Ben Kelly created a colourful, imaginative and flexible team environment in a light-industrial space. The new-look organisation now had the right type of base from which to influence opinion formers.

By the time there was a change of government in May 1997, the Design Council was 'back in the room'. Within weeks of Prime Minister Tony Blair entering 10 Downing Street, Sorrell and Summers were asked to organise an evening reception for Britain's leading designers. Out of this event came an initiative called Creative Britain, which gave the Council a pivotal role in exploring how the UK's strengths in design, creativity and innovation could enhance Britain's image internationally.

TOP Prime Minister Tony Blair launching the Design Council initiative Millennium Products at BBC Television Centre, 1999 (left); John Sorrell with Foreign Secretary Robin Cook at a Design Council event in Birmingham, 1998 (right)

ABOVE Millennium Products boat launch at Greenwich, December 1999

Later that year, the prime minister launched a new Design Council initiative called Millennium Products at BBC Television Centre. The aim was to identify outstanding examples of British innovation in design, science and technology by the year 2000. It was an exciting and ambitious undertaking that culminated on 14 December 1999 with Tony Blair and his entourage travelling by boat to the Millennium Dome site at Greenwich to announce the final tranche of Millennium Products, taking the number to around 1,000 innovations.

The 1990s thus closed on the highest of notes for the Design Council after such a difficult start to the decade. John Sorrell stood down as chairman in 2000 having, in his words, 'reintroduced design to all levels of government'. The organisation's work was part of a rebranding of Britain in an age of rapid globalisation, reminding the rest of the world of the UK's unique design strengths.

1   Deyan Sudjic, 'Made for the Millennium', *The Guardian* (28 September 1993).
2   *The Future Design Council*, report to Lord Strathclyde (London: Design Council, 1994).

ABOVE   Ben Kelly, Design Council office interior, Bow Street, London, 1997. Kelly is one of the UK's most influential designers, best known for his interior design of the legendary nightclub, The Haçienda, in Manchester

Design in the Digital Age: The Globalisation of the Creative Industries
Lynda Relph-Knight

The tone for any decade, however we choose to badge it, is set in the years immediately before. For the 1990s, it was arguably the fall of the Berlin Wall on 9 November 1989 that signified a new sense of openness and optimism across Europe, including in the UK. British students joined the tourist horde flocking to Germany to witness this momentous occasion and claim their souvenir chunk of concrete from the demolition site.

For many young designers, it would be their first trip abroad, though – not many years later – they'd find themselves working increasingly for clients from the Continent, particularly in packaging and branding, as European markets opened up following the Maastricht Treaty of 1992. Maastricht established the European Union, and Continental businesses joined the myriad of multinationals courting mainly London-based consultancies to create branding to make their products more appealing globally.

This European focus was amplified by the Barcelona Olympics, also in 1992. Again, there was cause for optimism and for travel elsewhere in Europe from the UK. And, as ever, design played its part. Josep Maria Trias's simple logo for the games set a tone of joy and freedom that was echoed in Javier Mariscal's unforgettable Cobi mascot.

A change in outlook was happening everywhere. When I joined *Design Week* in April 1989, my team used typewriters. There wasn't a computer in sight, and only a few design groups could afford an Apple Mac in the studio. It was all Letraset and Grant enlargers for sizing images back then. Hand-drawing was essential to communicate ideas, and typesetting a revered skill.

Nor could we Google information – there was no internet, no email. Our stories were gleaned over the phone or through face-to-face interviews; designers compiled mood boards from brochures and glossy magazine clippings; and professional photography was thriving for mugshots, pack shots and promotions. The use of recycled paper was an early nod to sustainability.

But technological change was on the horizon – and, when it hit us, we didn't look back. We'd had personal computers since the mid-1980s – the early Apple Macintosh, Amstrad and Apricot – but the advent of the Apple iMac in 1998 opened up a new concept of stylish portable models for home and studio.

As for mobile phones, the 'bricks' of the 1980s gave way to sleeker styling as technology developed to allow greater miniaturisation. Nokia and Ericsson were the big names in handsets, designed largely in-house. The launch of the Orange mobile network in 1994 made phones more user-friendly. Their distinctive branding, by Wolff Olins, featured simple sans serif typeface Helvetica and clear wording to help customers cut through technical jargon. This accessible approach was similar in tone to Apple's communications.

At the start of the decade, UK design was peppered with tiny ateliers, each specific to a particular design discipline – graphics, product or interiors mainly. Invariably, the name of the founder was over the door, and the sector was largely London-centric.

Pentagram had broken the mould, being a transatlantic multidisciplinary partnership, and was revered as such.

ABOVE European Union flag, 1992. Originally designed in 1955 for the Council of Europe, the flag became the official symbol of the EU following the Maastricht Treaty in 1992. Its twelve gold stars on a blue field represent unity, solidarity and harmony among European nations

Every consultancy wanted to be like Pentagram. Terence Conran, Michael Peters, Rodney Fitch, Stewart McColl and Wally Olins (with Michael Wolff), meanwhile, formed the pillars on which design was to be built as a multidisciplinary international business sector, spawning many a separate creative consultancy as their fortunes shifted over time. Designers led, though, and creativity was still key throughout the 1990s, before globalisation really took hold and the 'suits' gained prominence in burgeoning marketing services groups like WPP.

The opening up of European markets, following the Maastricht Treaty of 1992, fuelled a raft of consultancy takeovers as international supergroups were formed. American giants wanted a foothold in Europe and the UK was an old design ally – though we in the UK still looked to the USA for our models, especially in branding and retail design. London, in particular, was considered worldwide as a creative leader. British creative education was seen globally as second to none – a reputation it retains, though not with quite the same intensity.

As for the creative disciplines, 'corporate identity' – a phrase coined by Wolff Olins' co-founder Wally Olins in the 1980s – developed into the now ubiquitous 'branding', gradually taking packaging with it as part of the deal with clients. Retail grew, as high streets flourished and commercial chains expanded. Fashion and lifestyle stores had become a given in the 1980s – Next, The Body Shop and Habitat, for example. But now there were new names – Japanese 'no brand' store Muji opened in London in 1991, wine stores like Nicolas thrived, and bookstores like Borders and Waterstones installed coffee shops to keep customers lingering, reading and, of course, buying.

Towards the middle of the decade, digital design emerged in what became known as the 'dot-com boom'. Entrepreneurial designers like Simon Waterfall and Daljit Singh became the 'rock stars' of a burst of digital design groups that made emerging technologies palatable to ordinary folk through well-considered websites and by adding to clients' branding portfolios. Waterfall co-founded Deepend with Gary Lockton and David Streek in 1994, while Singh set up Digit in 1996.

Acquisitions were rife among digital groups, as consultancies across disciplines found they needed to offer digital services, which they would later integrate into the whole consultancy. The digital sector was to take a big hit in the dot-com bust following the 9/11 terrorist attacks in America, but it inevitably bounced back and now dominates communication design and retail. You can't halt the charge of technology.

Air travel proved another lucrative stream for branding and interior designers. The launch of easyJet in 1995 saw another, cheaper airline rivalling Ryanair and 'challenger brand' Virgin Atlantic. Design fed rivalry between airlines through lounges, plane interiors, ticketing and promotions.

Product design was already global, in line with bigger multinational clients. But the formation of IDEO in 1991 – when London's Moggridge Associates (set up by interface-design pioneer Bill Moggridge) and ID Two merged with David Kelley Design in San Francisco and with Matrix Product Design, set up in Palo Alto by British designer

LEFT   Josep Maria Trias, Olympic logo, 1992
ABOVE   Wolff Olins, Orange branding, 1994
OPPOSITE   Daljit Singh and interactive designers at Digit, *The Digital Aquarium*, 1995. Jointly developed with Motorola, the installation was shown in the Design Museum Tank, the public exhibition space outside on the museum's riverfront terrace

Mike Nuttall – moved the discipline into new realms of influence, harnessing industrial design, technology and design thinking.

Transport design was also in its heyday. The first Eurostar trains started to run through the Channel Tunnel in 1994, creating a convenient route to Europe for passengers, cars and freight. They were an Anglo-French design, with Jones Garrard creating the engine and French designer Roger Tallon designing the carriages.

The Eurostar Terminal, Waterloo International, a purpose-designed glass structure integrated into London's Waterloo Station, was designed by architect Nicholas Grimshaw and Partners. Grimshaw completed the refurbishment of Paddington Station as well, just before the decade was out. The Heathrow Express fast service between London's Paddington Station and Heathrow Airport launched in 1998, with identity and livery by Wolff Olins.

'Boutique' hotels were born of this move towards travel and leisure. French designer Philippe Starck continued his seminal work for American hotelier Ian Schrager with New York's Paramount Hotel, which opened in 1991. Starck and Schrager's collaboration eventually hit London with St Martins Lane Hotel, which opened in 1999, and the Sanderson a year later.

Workplace design was likewise key. From City dealing rooms to shared 'hot-desking' offices, there was a boom in environments that were flexible and comfortable. Office furniture design got a boost with the launch of Herman Miller's groundbreaking Aeron Chair in 1994. Its American designers, Bill Stumpf and Don Chadwick, used ergonomics to make the chair adjustable.

While all this was happening, design was starting to be taken seriously by client businesses and the UK government.

As Jeremy Myerson outlines in his introduction to this chapter, the Design Council found new direction under the Labour government of Tony Blair, which came to power in 1997. Designer Sir John Sorrell, appointed as chairman of the Council the same year by the then Tory Design Minister Baroness Denton of Wakefield, refocused its remit to encompass the public sector, business and education. A host of programmes such as Business Link and Design in Business Week sought to introduce design to small businesses as a generator of wealth and growth.

Blair 'got it' that design could improve business and enhance Britain's international reputation. He espoused design in the government's 'Cool Britannia' campaign from 1997 – hosting events for designers at 10 Downing Street and Buckingham Palace, and inviting design students to create gifts for influential foreign visitors and the like.

Starting in the previous decade, the 1990s were undoubtedly a time of superstar designers. The likes of Tom Dixon, Sir James Dyson, Ron Arad and Jasper Morrison were internationally acclaimed and the companies they created remain so. They joined fashion designers like Alexander McQueen, Matthew Williamson and the innovative Hussein Chalayan, all British-educated, on the world stage, alongside the supermodels, footballers and chefs of the day.

Elsewhere in the industry, 'design representation' was a phrase being bandied about in the early 1990s after then President of the Board of Trade Michael Heseltine said he would only deal with one spokesperson for each sector of industry. In response, the Chartered Society of Designers

LEFT   Glinting in the sunlight, the roof of Waterloo International station in London still under construction, c.1992

(CSD), representing individual designers; the burgeoning trade body the Design Business Association (DBA); the Design Council, and *Design Week* hatched a plan to create a single representative body.

The Halifax Initiative convened to thrash out the details in the mid-1990s resulted in Design Unity. This comprised the CSD, DBA, Design Council, Design Museum, creative educational charity D&AD and the Royal Society for the Encouragement of Arts, Manufactures and Commerce. Given the conflicting interests of its components – notably regarding lucrative awards schemes, education grants and sponsorship – the venture was doomed to failure. It did, however, lead to greater collaboration between the various bodies.

Towards the end of the decade, inclusive design started to be recognised in the UK though the work of Roger Coleman, who founded DesignAge within the Royal College of Art in 1992. DesignAge merged with the Helen Hamlyn Centre for Design in 1999 and broadened its remit beyond designing 'for our future selves' to take on health and well-being generally.

During this period, design management emerged as a career path. Marketing and design graduates were appointed by businesses to commission and manage the design of products and communications. Colleges such as Brunel, Staffordshire and De Montfort offered degree courses following the lead of the Royal College of Art and London Business School. Naomi Gornick championed such courses through her pioneering work.

While the design industry's dream of a designer on every company board has yet to be realised, prominent

ABOVE	Wolff Olins, Heathrow Express branding, 1999
BELOW	Philippe Starck et al., St Martins Lane Hotel interior, 1999

RIGHT Tom Dixon, Jack Light, 1996
OVERLEAF Richard Rogers, Millennium Dome, 1999. One of the largest of its type in the world, the dome was originally conceived as a Festival of Britain-type showcase to celebrate the third millennium

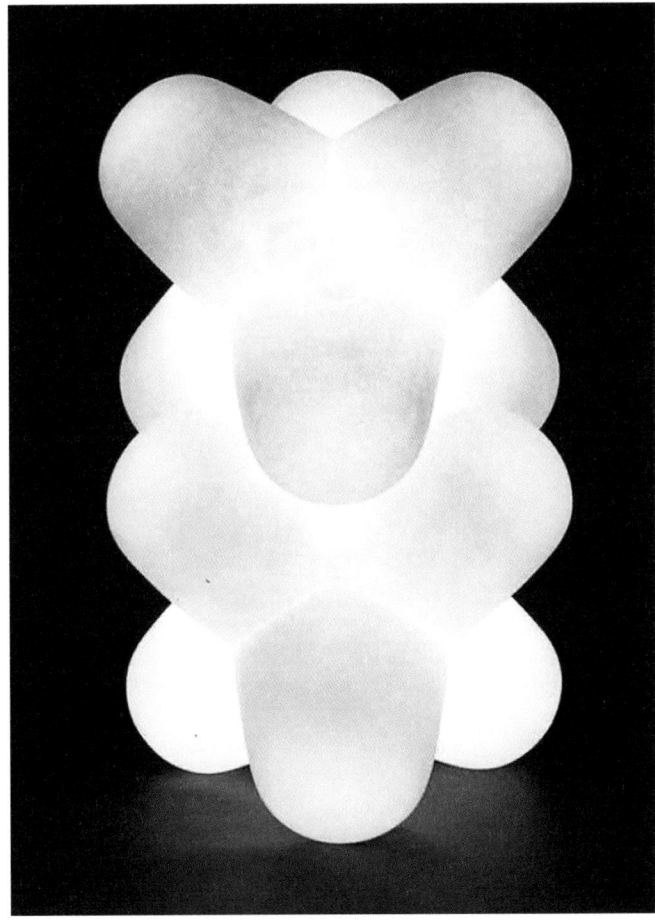

examples were showing through in the 1990s. At a national level, the likes of design consultants Wolff Olins founder Michael Wolff and Pentagram partner John McConnell were advising companies like stationery retailer W. H. Smith and the high street chemist Boots. More significantly, British designer Jonathan Ive – designer of the Apple iMac, iPhone and iPad – rose to Senior Vice-President of Industrial Design for technology giant Apple towards the end of the decade, having risen through the ranks since he joined as a designer in 1992.

Just as the Great Exhibition of 1851 and the Festival of Britain of 1951 sought to showcase British design, so the impending millennium afforded the opportunity to promote UK talent. More than 1,000 'Millennium Products' were selected by the Design Council in the late 1990s for display on the Greenwich Peninsula, a post-industrial site in southeast London.

The products were housed in a demountable pavilion designed by architect Allford Hall Monaghan Morris and commissioned by the Design Council and British Council. It contained video screens set in four inflatable 'wings', created by Inflate. Once the show ended, the exhibition was transported across the world, showcasing British design.

A key difference between this cache of designs and the items on display at previous expositions was that they weren't all objects. They were to show 'imagination, ingenuity and inspiration'. There was, for example, a system to purify or desalinate water in areas where drinking water is scarce.

The products sat alongside the Millennium Dome (now the O2 Arena). Designed by architect Richard Rogers and his then partner Mike Davies, the dome contained fourteen zones signifying 'Who we are', 'What we do' and 'Where we live', with installations created by various designers.

On the whole, the 1990s was a decade of transition in design, fuelled largely by technological advances and increased globalisation. Recessions came and went, but design battled on to change or respond to the way we conduct our lives and businesses. Many of the seeds sown then have blossomed – inclusive design and concerns with sustainability are notable examples. And while the high street may have lost its gloss, digital transactions feature in every sector, designed to convey a brand's values and make it easier for customers to engage. Design is now a university subject and recognised more as a vital investment than as purely a cost.

Subsequently, the noughties dawned on a high note with the Millennium celebrations. Who could foretell what was to happen in the new century?

OPPOSITE Don Chadwick and Bill Stumpf, Aeron chair, 1994. A seminal American design by Herman Miller, the Aeron chair redefined ergonomic seating with its mesh construction and adaptable support, inspiring a generation of British and international designers

ABOVE Deepend and designer Fred Flade, New Beetle website, c.1999. Deepend won numerous awards, including from the BIMA, LIAA and Silver D&AD. Its work is shown here on the original iMac, designed by Jonathan Ive for Apple in 1998, a product that revolutionised computer design with its translucent casing and bold use of colour

LIBERTY.

OPPOSITE Vanessa, 1990

Vanessa
Japanese Influence in a Global Era

This hand-painted artwork titled Vanessa, created for the Liberty Autumn/Winter 1990 collection, showcases a captivating array of Asian-inspired florals. Majestic chrysanthemums take centre stage within a lush botanical tapestry brimming with roses, peonies, blossoms, hydrangeas, berries and fruits. Delicately rendered with defined outlines, the flowers contrast beautifully with the dark background, enhancing their vibrant colours and intricate details.

Liberty's long-standing respect and passion for Japanese design has been a defining influence throughout its history. In 1889, Emma Liberty and her husband Arthur embarked on a journey to Japan that deepened their admiration for the country's creative traditions and exceptional artisanship. Emma, a keen photographer, documented their travels in a series of photographs, later compiled into a leather-bound journal now preserved in our archive. This enduring bond inspired the establishment of a Tokyo office and design studio in the 1990s, where the company continued to honour its heritage through Asian-inspired designs.

The 2000s

Design for a New Millennium

The Business of Design: The Design Council's Strategic Evolution
Ellie Runcie

The 2000s was a turbulent decade across the world – economically volatile, beginning with the dot-com bubble bursting in 2000 and ending with a major recession. Despite these challenges, the period saw considerable investment in business support through policies promoting local growth, with funds channelled through newly established Regional Development Agencies (RDAs). Public services increasingly recognised the importance of prevention and early intervention to address unsustainable demand.

British design was remarkably resilient and adaptable during this time. Not only did it show how innovation and cross-sector collaboration could fuel economic growth, it also developed solutions to social and environmental challenges. The Design Council was pivotal in this evolution, leading the agenda with programmes that showcased the transformative potential of design for businesses, public services and local communities.

These efforts resulted in 'design demonstrators' – scalable design methodologies that influenced thousands of organisations and laid a foundation for the following decade.

The value of design

The new century began with Millennium Products, a celebration of British creativity featuring more than 1,000 innovative designs. Launched at the Millennium Dome in December 1999 by Prime Minister Tony Blair, it attracted significant global attention. Building on this success, the Design Council unveiled *Great Expectations* in 2001, a touring exhibition that included notable highlights from the Millennium Products showcase. The centrepiece was a 54-metre banquet table of 100 objects that represented the best in British design, including Marks Barfield Architects' London Eye, Marion Deuchars' repackaging for Penguin of George Orwell's novels, the Bioform bra by Seymour Powell Design Consultancy, Thomas Heatherwick's Plank chair and Lambie-Nairn's BBC2 brand idents. The exhibition began at New York's Grand Central Station, before touring internationally.

OPPOSITE Casson Mann, *Great Expectations* exhibition, 2001. This award-winning exhibition was part of the UKinNY festival and was based in Grand Central Station, New York

PREVIOUS PAGE Marks Barfield Architects, London Eye, 2000. Originally conceived as a temporary installation, the London Eye redefined modern engineering with its cable-tensioned structure and was the world's tallest observation wheel at its completion

Eager to broaden the narrative around British design, the Council highlighted its impact beyond aesthetics and functionality, focusing on its strategic value for businesses. The 2004 Design Index revealed that FTSE-listed businesses that prioritised design outperformed others by 200 per cent over ten years. This finding caught the attention of the Council's sponsor, the Department of Trade and Industry (DTI), whose funding allowed the Council to expand its initiatives.

In 2002, the Council launched the Design Demonstrators programme, using pilot projects to explore how design could address strategic challenges in businesses (particularly technology start-ups and small- and medium-sized enterprises [SMEs] in manufacturing) and public services. Over three years, more than 100 organisations participated, generating insights that informed broader design approaches.

A key outcome of this work was the Double Diamond framework, introduced in 2004. This methodology categorised the design process in four phases – Discover, Define, Develop and Deliver – and became a key tool for strategic innovation. Illustrated with two intersecting diamonds, the first focused on discovering the problem to be addressed while the second focused on developing the right solution. Released under a Creative Commons licence, it was widely adopted by the design community and beyond.

By the mid-2000s, the Council was also examining the success of Silicon Valley start-ups and contributed to an influential report, 'Innovating through People-Centred Design – Lessons from the USA'. This work underscored the potential of user-centred design to drive innovation.

In 2005, Chancellor Gordon Brown commissioned the Cox Review to examine the role of design in the UK economy. It highlighted the findings of the Council's Design Demonstrators programme and recommended introducing its initiatives at a national scale. This led to the government's £10 million investment in a new programme called Designing Demand.

Democratising design

Designing Demand aimed to help UK businesses use design strategically to drive growth. The programme, built around the Double Diamond, guided businesses

OPPOSITE The Design Council's visual representation of its Double Diamond design and innovation process, 2003

BELOW Design demonstration: Owlstone's nanotech device, 2002. It went on to become a cancer diagnostic breathalyser ten years later, 2002

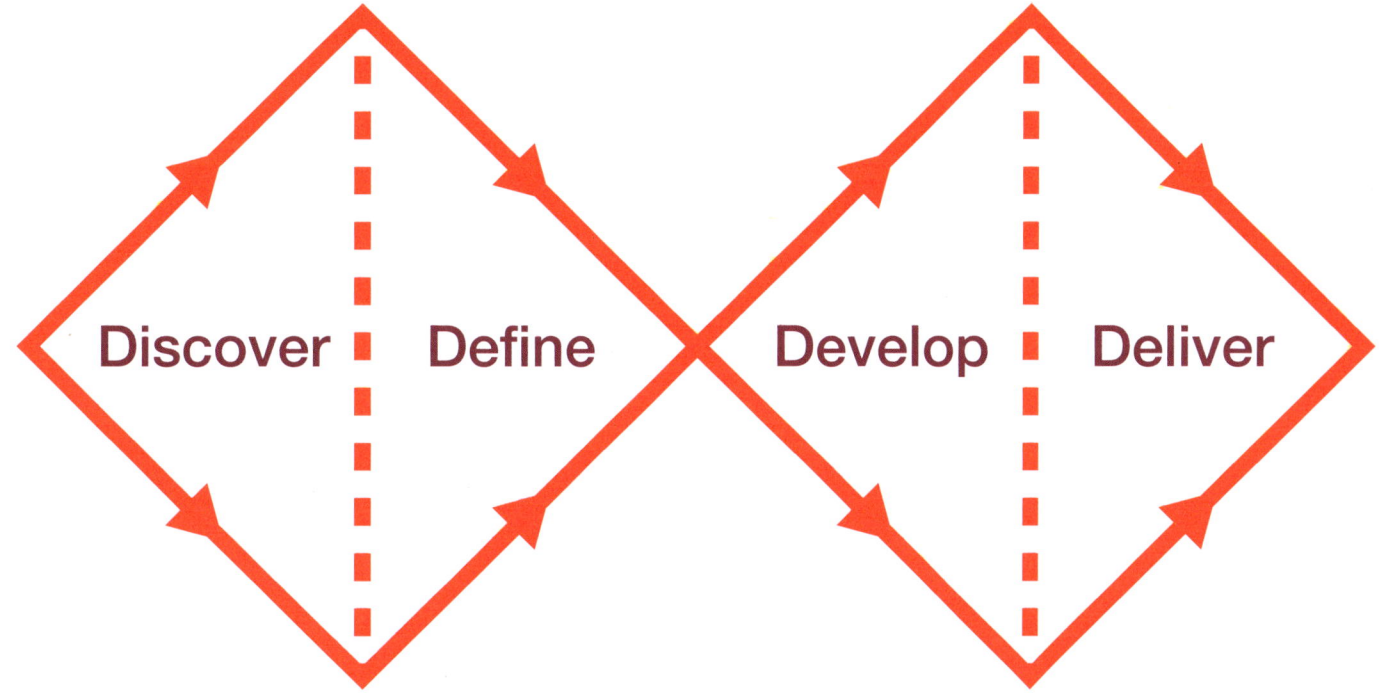

ABOVE Naylor Industries, Yorkshire Flowerpots range, 2006. Launched into a market where British manufactured products had been largely displaced by poor-quality pots from cheap-labour countries

to identify their needs, create design briefs and collaborate with designers. Delivered in partnership with RDAs, it targeted businesses unfamiliar with design but with high growth potential, effectively creating new markets for the design industry.

By 2010, over 5,000 businesses across the UK had participated, leading to new products, services, brands and business models. The programme had a measurable impact: for every £1 invested in design, businesses saw more than £20 in revenue, £4 in profit and more than £5 in exports. Additionally, 91 per cent of participating businesses survived the 2008 recession, compared with 49 per cent of a control group. By the programme's end, businesses that used design strategically for the first time had generated £56 million in revenue.

The Council continued to explore design's broader applications, publishing the report 'Eleven Lessons' in 2007. It analysed how leading companies – including Alessi, BT Group, LEGO, Microsoft, Sony, Starbucks, Virgin Atlantic, Whirlpool, Xerox and Yahoo – integrated design into their processes. The findings provided practical insights for designers and business leaders alike.

Expanding the approach

The 2008 recession prompted the Design Council to establish an in-house research and development team, RED, to explore how design could address societal issues. This led to the launch of Designs of the Time (Dott) in the northeast of the UK, funded by the local RDA. The programme brought designers together with communities and service providers to tackle challenges such as dementia, sexual health, schools and unemployment. Its success led to a second iteration in the southwest of the country in 2009.

Another notable project, Design Bugs Out, aimed to reduce hospital infections by designing easy-to-clean medical equipment. Launched in partnership with the Department of Health and the NHS Purchasing and Supply Agency, it resulted in four products – a commode, a blood-pressure cuff, a bedside cabinet and a patient chair – that were adopted by hospitals nationwide.

OPPOSITE Bristol Maid, eClean bedside cabinet, 2009 (top); Pearson Lloyd and Kirton Healthcare Group, DBO commode, 2009 (bottom). Part of the Design Bugs Out initiative, the cabinet's open, backless design minimises dirt traps and improves accessibility, while the commode's simplified construction and smooth surfaces enhance cleanability in healthcare settings

RIGHT Pearson Lloyd and Kirton Healthcare Group Ltd, Patient Chair, 2009. Designed for the Design Bugs Out initiative, this moulded plastic chair features waterproof padding, ergonomic support and smooth surfaces to enhance comfort and reduce infection risks

These initiatives demonstrated how design could drive innovation in public services and healthcare, laying the groundwork for future programmes.

Building on the success of Designing Demand, the Design Council expanded its approach to public services in 2008, collaborating with organisations like Lewisham Council to rethink how design could tackle service pressures. These projects demonstrated that user-centred design not only generated innovative solutions but also reduced costs, laying the groundwork for wider adoption in the next decade.

Making the case for the Design Council

The Design Council's evidence-based approach proved crucial during the Coalition Government's 2010 Temple Review, which evaluated all publicly funded organisations. The review endorsed the Council's impact and recommended its continuation under a revised operating model.

Despite widespread funding cuts, Designing Demand was retained and continued to support businesses into the next decade. Additionally, the Council merged with the Commission for Architecture and the Built Environment (CABE), becoming Design Council CABE and transitioning to charity status.

A decade of reframing design

The 2000s was a transformative period for the Design Council. By reframing design as a user-centred, experience-driven practice, it unlocked new ways to address systemic challenges. Its open sharing of the Double Diamond and its commitment to building a robust evidence base cemented its reputation as a leader in design innovation. This decade not only expanded the role of design in business and public services but also strengthened the Council's ability to navigate the growing political and economic uncertainties of the 2010s and beyond.

New Century, New Design: Britain's Creative Transformation
Max Fraser

The Cool Britannia optimism of the late 1990s paved the way for an energetic start to the new millennium, embodied by the significant Millennium Dome on London's Greenwich Peninsula, designed by Richard Rogers. The vast purpose-built structure housed exhibits that looked at Britain's future in science, technology and design, aimed at spurring on a future of pioneering innovation in the UK.

Around this time, there was a broader embrace of this thing called 'design'. The word had often been linked to the fashion business, but now fashion was rubbing shoulders with furniture and product design – and attracting mainstream attention.

Hospitality design was having its moment: the era of restaurant entrepreneurs such as Oliver Peyton was in full swing. His portfolio was marked by the lavish Atlantic Bar & Grill, Coast, Mash and Inn the Park in London, as well as Mash & Air in Manchester, given strong design identity by the likes of Marc Newson, Tom Dixon and Andy Martin Architecture. The Social, designed by David Adjaye, became a central London drinking hotspot.

Meanwhile, the Terence Conran restaurant empire was sizeable, bolstered in this decade by the additions of Boundary and its associated restaurant-café Albion in east London, as well as Lutyens in the City of London. Hyper-cool hotels St Martins Lane and Sanderson were the places to stay at the start of the millennium, designed as they were with theatrical interiors by Philippe Starck.

In parallel, the popular press was lapping up the latest in design. Sunday newspaper supplements and magazines like *Wallpaper** were commissioning glamorous photoshoots that gave the same billing to furniture as they did to outfits. Voyeuristic glimpses into contemporary homes were the mainstay of many magazines, among them *ELLE Decoration* and *Livingetc*. And publishers were churning out books about home improvements and contemporary lifestyle hacks, as well as showing a fascination with open-plan loft living.

Across these titles, the celebration and awareness of a new generation of individual designers was gaining traction. Many of them could be found exhibiting their prototype designs at trade events such as 100% Design in London. Established in 1995, this annual show was dedicated to contemporary designers and manufacturers, and rapidly became an essential launchpad into the burgeoning contemporary design market. Here, young designers showed alongside the more established, which made it a place for talent to be discovered but also for orders to be placed.

At a time when dial-up internet was still the norm and websites were rudimentary, printed media and physical exhibitions were the conduits to communicate the energy that was carrying the UK's products and domestic goods out from the beige era of the 1990s into a time of greater optimism and aesthetic bravery.

There was a generation of designers using platforms like 100% Design to showcase their newly founded studios, displaying objects underpinned with a healthy dose of experimentation and British wit. Designers like Carl Clerkin, Michael Marriott, Gitta Gschwendtner, JAM, Tom Kirk, Tord Boontje, Timorous Beasties and Alexander Taylor took

ABOVE Tom Dixon, Mirror Ball Pendant, 2003. Inspired by space helmets and disco balls, this highly reflective pendant light is designed to blend into its surroundings by mirroring its environment

it on themselves to exhibit prototypes with the express aim of attracting manufacturers.

Those less keen on the booth format (and prices) of trade fairs embraced alternative platforms at the same time as 100% Design. Designersblock became the enfant terrible of exhibitions, bringing together international designers in disused London buildings or those about to undergo development. These and other smaller exhibitions made up a growing fringe festival in late September, first embraced by 100% Design – and branded 100% Guaranteed – before the establishment of the London Design Festival in 2003.

Founded by John Sorrell and Ben Evans, the Festival started out with a conference called the 'World Creative Forum', a lofty event with an even loftier ticket price that was ultimately out of reach for many of the target audience. Over subsequent years, the Festival morphed into an umbrella marketing organisation for a growing fortnight of creative celebrations that also included Open House for architecture and London Fashion Week, which usually dominated the press headlines.

It's no coincidence that the property market was enjoying considerable growth at the back end of the 1990s. Homeowners were benefiting from cheap credit and considerable value gains, unlocking a fortuitous generation able to invest in design.

The UK's independent retailers of furniture and interior products were also benefiting from this uptick in interest, making many new contemporary designs available to an increasingly susceptible and affluent audience.

Profiting from this perfect storm were the European manufacturing brands (mostly Italian), whose UK agents

OPPOSITE   Rogers Stirk Harbour + Partners, Terminal 5, Heathrow, 2008 (top); Amanda Levete, Prototile, 2007. Designed for the London Design Festival's Size + Matter series, this installation featured a curving wall of approximately 220 interlocking DuPont Corian tiles, showcasing the material's versatility through thermoforming techniques (middle); Jasper Morrison, Crate Series Daybed, 2007. Part of Morrison's Crate Series, this daybed is crafted from waxed yellow pine, reflecting his philosophy of elevating everyday objects through functional design

RIGHT   Christopher Kane, Central Saint Martins MA graduate collection, 2006. Kane's breakout collection featured bold neon hues and body-conscious silhouettes, marking him as one of British fashion's most promising new talents

were exhibiting their creations and advertising them in the magazines, while the media wrote about them and the shops stocked them. Brands such as B&B Italia, Zanotta, Cappellini, Living Divani, Magis, Kartell, Flos and Artemide were riding high, supported by retailers such as The Conran Shop, twentytwentyone, SCP, Viaduct, Geoffrey Drayton and Aram.

While product imports were growing, British manufacturers of contemporary furniture were few and far between. There was not enough business in the UK to support the growing numbers of talented designers graduating from its universities, so attentions shifted abroad. British design talent became our export.

This had started a decade earlier: British designer Jasper Morrison began his relationship with Swiss furniture manufacturer Vitra with his Plywood Chair (1989); Tom Dixon's S-Chair (1991) was picked up by Italian producer Cappellini; the Loop Table (1996) by Barber Osgerby was also taken on by Cappellini, having been spotted at 100% Design; the Tom Vac chair (1999) by Ron Arad went into production with Vitra.

These European stalwart brands gave individual designers strong publicity and a reputational boost at the globally attended Milan Design Week, something more and more designers were eager to achieve. Building on the era of designer celebrity that began to emerge in the 1980s, these international showcases gave even greater prominence to talented designers, with their names shining in lights and the media eager for interviews, ushering in an era of designer as celebrity (albeit mostly in industry circles).

It wasn't by chance that these designers were attracting attention: the strength of the UK's design schools was producing an experimental yet commercially minded generation of designers. The spirit of cross-disciplinary experimentation at institutions such as the Royal College of Art (RCA) and Central Saint Martins (CSM) made them magnets for domestic as well as international designers. Their graduate shows were must-visit events for talent scouts.

In tandem, the government was waking up to the creative industries' growing contribution to the UK economy, adding energy to an expansion of design courses. Subjects like product design, graphics and fashion saw increased enrolment from students, and schools diversified their offerings to include specialist courses in everything from service design, interaction design, web design, UX/UI and sustainability. Technology took hold with students embracing digital fabrication, computer-aided design, 3D printing and graphic software.

As much as students and qualified designers were eager to transform their ideas into products and services, the growing burden of newness was increasingly playing its part in eroding the natural world and our climate. By no means a new problem, climate change was nevertheless baring its teeth with greater ferocity in this decade, and society was waking up.

Drought and wildfires, as well as flooding and superstorms, were devastating localities across the world with greater frequency. Reliant on fossil fuels, humanity's pervasive material appetite was driving extractive behaviour well beyond what the planet could sustain and was leaving a

trail of waste and pollution in its path. It rapidly became a topic that took hold in the education system and the practising design industry; the emphasis on environmental and societal challenges was addressed with greater urgency.

This was by no means unique to the UK, with rich nations across the world starting to question their incessant consumption. In turn, designers and manufacturers began to pay greater attention to eco-friendly materials and production techniques, circular-economy principles and life-cycle analysis. A lot of that shift could be deemed superficial but, at a minimum, attitudes were changing. For example, in 2003 the charity Bioregional focused on our ecological footprint, launching the One Planet Living framework with the World Wide Fund for Nature (WWF), providing a roadmap for sustainable living and influencing architecture, product design and urban planning.

The severe floods of summer 2007 acted as a reminder that the UK's temperate climate was not immune to environmental disruption. Responding to growing concerns, the government passed the Climate Change Act in 2008, establishing the world's first legally binding framework for reducing greenhouse gas emissions, a significant shift in how Britain approached the climate crisis.

However, just as the nation was embracing its role in combating climate change, the September 2008 global financial crisis struck. The UK economy was devastated by the worldwide economic downturn. This period of instability rippled across all industries, tempering the risk-taking and experimentation that had fuelled a decade of vibrant creativity. The creatives remained, but their opportunities were dramatically scaled back.

In the years preceding the financial crash, the internet had expanded rapidly. As bandwidth and loading speeds increased, so too did the sophistication of websites. Individuals, collectives and companies could very quickly create updatable online portfolios of their work, in turn expanding their communicable reach worldwide. In parallel, e-commerce became a possibility for everyone, allowing greater autonomy and less reliance on the traditional routes to market. Media moved online too, with design and architecture websites such as designboom and Dezeen publishing news as soon as it broke.

For those independent designers eager to attract manufacturers to their creations, reaching them had got a lot easier. Furthermore, for those who were making their own pieces, suddenly direct sales via their own websites were possible. Ridding themselves of commission-hungry representatives or miserly royalties from the brands, more and more designers were able to self-produce, sell direct, and earn full margins and instant income. This is an approach we recognise more and more today.

With the uncertainty of the recession and the onset of the 'austerity' period of governance, many brands scaled back and became more conservative in the designs they commissioned. Nevertheless, there was still plenty of strong creativity to champion, as was embodied by the *Designs of the Year* exhibition at London's Design Museum, which launched in 2008. This annual exhibition rapidly became an important celebration of the most innovative and imaginative designs across a broad swathe of creative disciplines, including furniture, product, transport, graphics, fashion, architecture and digital. Each year's featured projects were

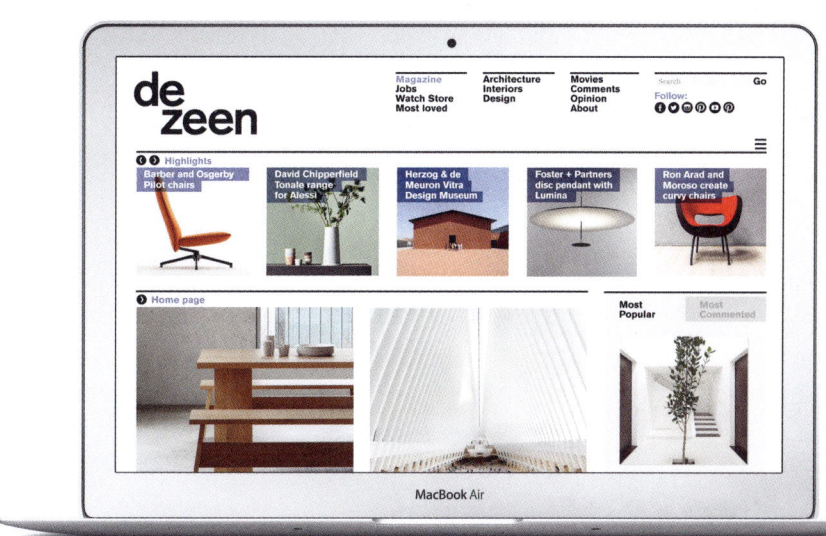

OPPOSITE Apple, iPhone, first model, 2007. Design led by Jonathan Ive (left); Ross Lovegrove, Tŷ Nant water bottle, 2001. Its rippled form, inspired by water, reflects Lovegrove's organic design approach, blending aesthetics with function (right)

RIGHT Dezeen, website designed by Micha Weidmann, 2007

PREVIOUS SPREAD Zaha Hadid, BMW Central Building, Leipzig, 2005. A fusion of architecture and industry, Hadid's BMW Leipzig plant redefines the factory as a fluid, interconnected workspace, blurring the line between production and office spaces

nominated by international design experts, and the collective exhibition provided a platform for projects that were making a significant impact on society and culture.

The decade may have ended with a slump in confidence as well as finances, but it's important to remind ourselves that the 2000s was marked by a great diversity of celebratory design and architecture moments. Along with the aforementioned Millennium Dome, 2000 welcomed the London Eye to the capital's skyline: Europe's largest cantilevered observation wheel, designed by Marks Barfield Architects, it was only ever intended to exist as a temporary structure. The next year, a disused china-clay pit in Cornwall became a hub for ecological education as the visionary Eden Project, centred around two geodesic domes designed by Nicholas Grimshaw and Partners (now known as Grimshaw Architects).

In 2002, furniture and product designer Tom Dixon launched a brand under his own name, successfully introducing the Mirror Ball Pendant light two years later. In 2004, the City of London's skyline evolved considerably when Foster + Partners' 30 St Mary Axe (affectionately known as 'The Gherkin') broke the conventions of corporate architecture. In the same year, having only completed four buildings, Iraqi–British architect Zaha Hadid made strides in her industry when she won the esteemed Pritzker Prize for Architecture.

London won the bid to host the 2012 Olympics in July 2005, prompting considerable regeneration and the rapid construction of the Olympic Park in Stratford in east London.

In the industrial-design world, British-born designer Jony Ive led the design team behind Apple's revolutionary iPhone, which was launched in 2007 and went on to dominate the touchscreen smartphone market. Dyson, the pioneer of vacuum cleaners, launched a new typology for electric hand dryers in 2006 with the Dyson Airblade, which are now ubiquitous worldwide.

Terminal 5 was added to London Heathrow in 2008, designed by Rogers Stirk Harbour + Partners to expand the capacity of one of the world's busiest airports. A couple of years later, maverick designer Thomas Heatherwick made his mark on the London streets with the launch of the New Routemaster bus, reviving the typology of the city's classic red double-decker bus for the twenty-first century. As London's population grew, the decade concluded with the start of construction on Crossrail, the capital's major east–west rail line that would become one of Europe's largest infrastructure projects.

Looking back, the 2000s were a transformative period for British design. The decade began with millennial optimism and a creative flourishing that saw British designers gain international recognition. Digital technologies revolutionised both the design process and how creative work reached its audience. However, the growing awareness of environmental challenges and the 2008 financial crisis prompted a fundamental shift in design thinking. As the decade closed, the industry had begun to balance innovation with sustainability, setting new priorities that would shape design practice for years to come.

LEFT — Hussein Chalayan, Readings Collection, Spring/Summer 2008. This collection featured innovative garments embedded with LED lights and Swarovski crystals, creating dynamic light displays that extended beyond the fabric, exemplifying Chalayan's fusion of fashion and technology

BELOW — Ron Arad, Victoria and Albert sofa, 2000. Designed for Moroso, this sculptural sofa features a continuous flow of curving lines, reflecting Arad's innovative approach to form and function. Named after the Victoria and Albert Museum, where an early version was exhibited, it exemplifies his fusion of art and industrial design

ABOVE Foster + Partners, 30 St Mary Axe ('The Gherkin'), London, 2004. A landmark of contemporary British architecture, its energy-efficient design and distinctive curved form redefined London's skyline

LIBERTY.

OPPOSITE Small Susanna, 2005

Small Susanna
A Modern Floral Classic

Originally hand-drawn in fineliner pen and painted in the Liberty design studio by the talented designer Emma Mawston, Small Susanna was created for the Liberty Spring/Summer 2005 collection. The design showcases intricate studies of sunflowers, arranged in a dense, multidirectional pattern. Small Susanna was then rescaled and recoloured for the 2008 seasonal range, before joining the Classics collection.

Mawston's signature style was a hallmark of the 2000s. As Head of Design at Liberty Fabrics, she crafted meticulous hand-drawn florals and bold yet delicate patterns that quickly achieved classic status. Her artistic passion shaped Liberty's print identity, fostering a studio culture of immersive research, sketching and on-site painting, with a strong emphasis on the symbolism of plants and flowers. Blending traditional techniques with modern design sensibilities, the collections of this era exude timeless yet contemporary appeal. Dramatic, large-scale artworks rich in texture and colour were often created in repeat by hand using mixed media, inspired by books, exhibitions, travel, nature and music.

The 2010s

Designing Through Uncertainty

Design Thinking in Action: The Design Council in a Changing World
Cat Drew

The 2010s was a tumultuous decade, beginning in the aftermath of the 2008 global economic crash and ending as COVID-19 loomed in a little-heard-of city called Wuhan. In the UK, Conservative governments grappled with the long-term effects of the financial crisis, drove increasing digitalisation across the public and private sectors, and oversaw a country at its peak of national pride during the 2012 Olympics yet deeply divided by the Brexit referendum that led to the nation's withdrawal from the European Union.

During this time, the Design Council concentrated on demonstrating and championing the value of design among commissioners in business and the public sector. This emphasis on increasing demand for design undoubtedly contributed to the continued growth of the design sector, from £56.4 billion gross value added (GVA) in 2010 to £97.4 billion in 2019. Over the same period, the design workforce expanded from 1.3 million people in 2010 to just under 2 million in 2019. Building on its mission to demonstrate design's worth across multiple sectors, the Council next turned its attention to revitalising businesses.

Design for business

Responding to the financial crash, the Design Council – led by David Kester as CEO – had already begun supporting SMEs to harness design to boost profits and productivity, creating more commercially attractive products and more efficient processes. This support was crucial, since many SMEs lacked both funding and in-house design expertise. In the following five years, the Council supported 5,000 SMEs, proving that investing in design yielded a 20:1 return on investment. Moreover, 91 per cent of businesses using design were still operating five years later, compared with 49 per cent who were not. Together with data from management consultancy McKinsey, this provided compelling evidence that design was good for business. Meanwhile, the design consultancy IDEO popularised 'design thinking', which made its way into the business world through MBA programmes and led to design agencies not only creating products for businesses but also teaching them how to think like designers.

PREVIOUS PAGE Led By Donkeys, Brexit SOS projection, 4 April 2019. Projected onto the White Cliffs of Dover, this large-scale protest highlighted Brexit uncertainty, featuring an SOS message alongside a quote from EU Council President Donald Tusk

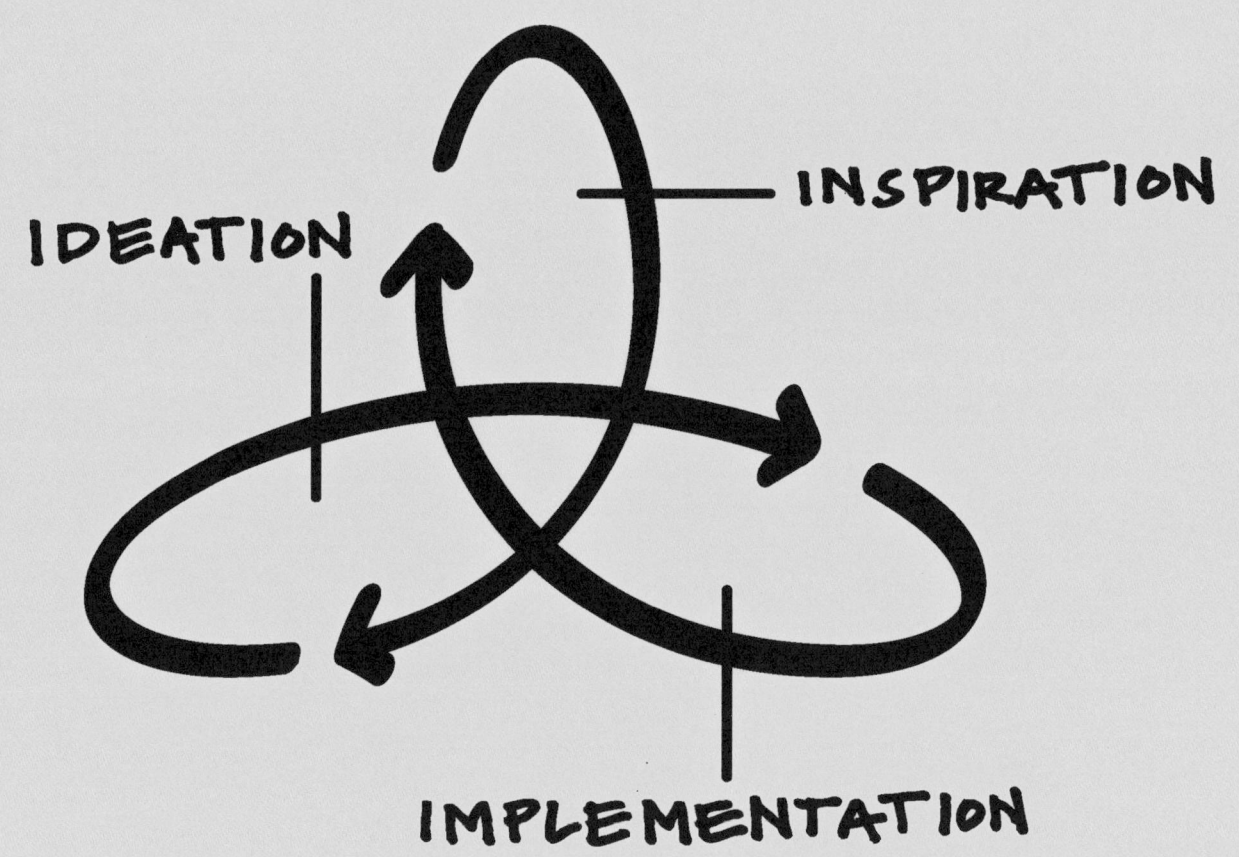

ABOVE   IDEO, The three core activities of design thinking, 2001

The Council's remit extended beyond traditional businesses to early start-ups and social enterprises. Under John Mathers (CEO of the Council from 2012 to 2016), the Spark programme – launched in 2015 and running until 2019 – encouraged innovators to use design in prototyping their early-stage ideas and bringing them to market. While many failed, one notable success was Rockit, a vibrating pacifier that clips to a pram to help a baby sleep, which has sold over 800,000 units worldwide and was the recipient of two Queen's Awards for Enterprise in 2022.

The programme Transform Ageing had a different focus, targeting social enterprises. Over three years, Design Council experts supported sixty-two social businesses across the southwest of England, helping them create products and services for people in later life, from forest bathing walks to a personal alarm watch. This approach gave local councils a new model for delivering adult services, while boosting the local economy. These businesses generated £3.7 million in local economic revenue, creating 193 jobs and 800 volunteering opportunities, and more than half of them were led by people in later life. By engaging local communities and emphasising the needs of users, Transform Ageing illustrated the Council's commitment to inclusive design that delivers both social and economic benefits, fundamentally changing how services could be provided and received.

Design in the public sector

Local, national and even supranational government bodies were eager to find new ways of working as they faced austerity and shrinking budgets. Lord Bichard, the Design Council chair, led the commission Restarting Britain, which investigated how human-centred design could improve public services.

At the local level, the Design Council partnered with the Local Government Association and the NHS on an ambitious programme to embed design thinking into council and health services. Over eight years, Design Council experts worked with 100 teams on various challenges, from children's services in Staffordshire to digital health checks in Suffolk and suicide prevention in Sussex.

BELOW The Rockit baby rocker, 2016 (top); Government Digital Service, GOV.UK website, 2012 (bottom)

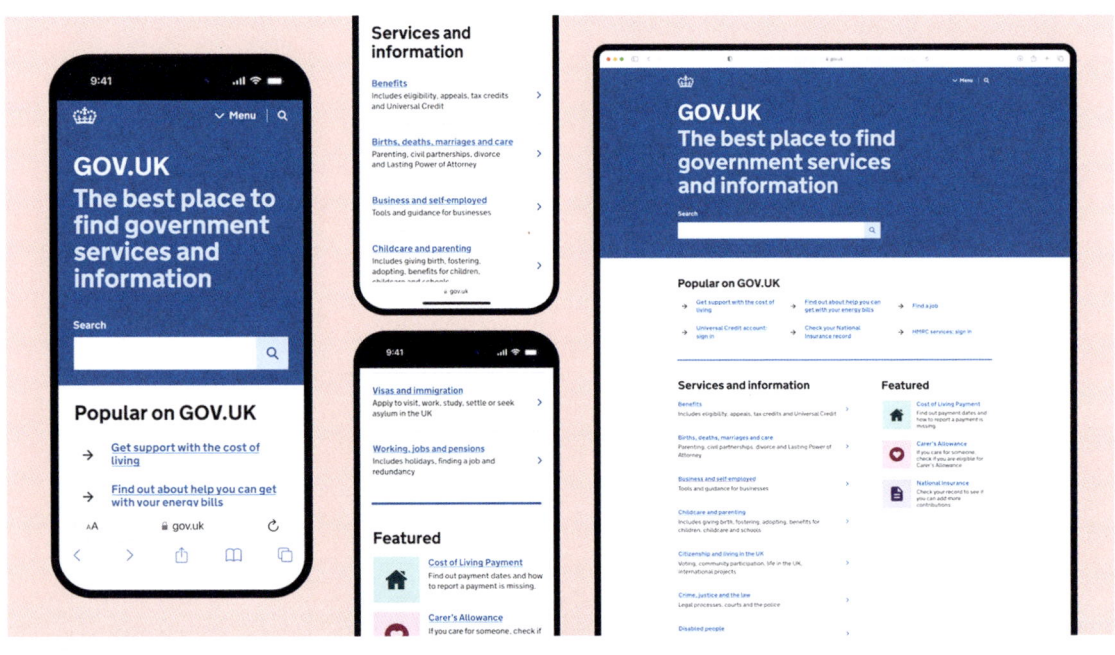

Alongside improving services for people, these initiatives upskilled local authority staff, who applied their new design knowledge to future projects. The surge in public-sector design demand helped to establish new consultancies, such as the Innovation Unit, Fjord, Snook, FutureGov and Uscreates – which were often acquired by larger firms like Accenture and Deloitte, attracted by the advantages of a user-centred approach.

At the national level, this inspired the creation of the Policy Lab, a small team in the Cabinet Office that introduced design thinking to government policymaking. One of its founders, Andrea Siodmok, had been the Design Council's Chief Design Officer, while the other (the current author) would later assume that role. Around the same time, the Government Digital Service used user-centred design to transform digital public services via GOV.UK. Spearheaded by Ben Terrett, Mike Bracken and Lou Downe, GOV.UK won the Design Museum's Design of the Year Award in 2013 and became a model for governments worldwide. It made bureaucracy – from renewing a passport to getting a divorce – a much smoother process and accessible to all users.

At the supranational level, the Design Council led the Design for Europe programme, a three-year initiative co-funded by the European Commission as part of its Action Plan for Design-Driven Innovation. Launched in January 2014, this programme fostered design-driven innovation across Europe through a consortium of 14 partners. The initiative developed an online platform to showcase design's role in innovation and organised more than 100 events across 54 European cities, including a significant design summit in Brussels in May 2015 that attracted over 200 delegates. Through the work of 47 design ambassadors across EU member states, the programme successfully encouraged 10 of the 28 EU countries to embrace design at national policy levels.

Design for place

For the Design Council, 2011–12 was significant not just for the London Olympics but also for its merger with the Commission for Architecture and the Built

ABOVE Government Digital Service, posters for Design Principles, 2012

Environment (CABE). This brought together design disciplines across the entire ecosystem, from digital products to urban infrastructure.

One of CABE's pioneering moves was establishing Design Review, a process in which a panel of design experts critiques and offers advice during stages of planning, examining issues such as accessibility and sustainability. Over the decade, the Design Council and its Built Environment Network of more than 400 Experts provided over 1,000 Design Reviews, improving projects of various scales across the country – from smaller schemes to larger undertakings. The Design Council also worked with national bodies such as Network Rail and Highways England, drawing on expert wisdom to inform government guidance on the built environment, including the National Planning Policy Framework and the National Model Design Code. These documents continue to influence how towns and cities are developed and connected. Building on these practical contributions to the built environment, the Council took a strategic view, too, of design's impact on the wider economy, leading to more nuanced research into its reach and challenges.

Celebrated worldwide, the 2012 Olympic Games became a showcase for British design and ingenuity, from the cutting-edge architecture of the venues to the ecological and economic regeneration of the Lea Valley into what is now the Queen Elizabeth Olympic Park. This legacy reshaped London's urban geography, shifting its centre of gravity eastwards for good. The Council played a significant role by reviewing every piece of construction within the Olympic Village to ensure the design quality, sustainability and long-term legacy of all new buildings and spaces associated with the Games – including temporary structures such as sponsors' pavilions, the stadium itself and masterplans for the future of the area. The Council partnered with the organising committee to launch a competition for the design and manufacture of the Olympic torch, which was won by Barber Osgerby. Their sleek industrial design later won the Design Museum's Design of the Year Award. Another Council initiative, Beyond 2012, celebrated the behind-the-scenes stories from designers who helped shape the Games.

ABOVE — Stella McCartney, Team GB belted jacket, 2012. Designed for the London 2012 Olympics with Adidas, this jacket reinterprets the Union Jack in blue and white with red accents, incorporating recycled materials in line with McCartney's commitment to sustainability (top); Barber Osgerby, London 2012 Olympic torch, 2011. A lightweight, perforated aluminium torch with 8,000 holes representing each torchbearer; its trilateral form symbolised London hosting the Games for a third time. It carried the bold, angular London 2012 logo, designed by Wolff Olins to reflect the Games' energy and inclusivity (bottom)

LEFT — Heatherwick Studio, London 2012 Olympic cauldron, 2012. Featuring 204 copper petals representing each competing nation, the cauldron's petals rose and converged to form a single flame, symbolising unity and collaboration

ABOVE Zaha Hadid, London Aquatics Centre, 2011. Designed for the London 2012 Olympics, the Aquatics Centre embodies Hadid's signature fluidity, with a sweeping wave-like roof inspired by water in motion. Now a public facility, it remains a landmark of contemporary British architecture

Design economy research – and diversity

Throughout the 2010s, the Design Council not only demonstrated the value of design through its projects but also honed its methods for capturing impact at a macro level. It revealed that design was widespread in non-design businesses, from automotive to retail and construction, and that an even larger group was using design skills and thinking in its work. While this points to design's growing presence across society, the sector still faced a serious diversity problem: seventy-eight per cent of designers were male, and the proportion of designers who were people of colour remained well below the UK average. These statistics raised pressing questions about representation and equity in design, prompting further initiatives to diversify the profession. Sarah Weir, the Council's first female CEO, championed greater inclusivity, supporting organisations like Design Can.

By the end of the decade, the Design Council had demonstrated how design could foster business growth, enable more efficient and inclusive public services, and improve health and well-being through digitalisation. These capabilities would soon be tested by the global COVID-19 pandemic, which arrived in early 2020. Having already demonstrated design's capacity to adapt to financial upheaval and social needs, the Council would soon confront an even more complex and challenging landscape: looming larger still was the challenge of the climate and nature crises, set to demand yet another innovative response from Britain's designers.

Design and Disruption in a Divided Britain
Mark Cortes Favis

The 2010s was a decade that no one could have prepared for. If the 2000s had been a time of confidence – defined by globalisation, expansion and digital optimism – the 2010s was the hangover: a decade of division, crisis and recalibration. Its powerful currents washed away the optimism of the past, pulling British design into deeper, more uncertain waters. The 2010s was the decade of the swipe and the scroll – of Instagram filters and fake news, of Tinder hookups and Grindr dates and Deliveroo dinners, of Hypebeast fashion and protest placards. Algorithms dictated taste, movements took shape in hashtags, and design became more democratic – yet more dangerous – than ever before.

This transformation came in waves of disruption: political instability, economic uncertainty, technological revolution and social upheaval. The 2008 recession cast the first stone, rippling across creative practice for years to come. As markets crumbled and confidence faltered, Britain entered a period of extraordinary political volatility, with four prime ministers and three general elections – a level of churn not seen since the 1970s. Against this backdrop, the Conservative-led coalition's austerity measures carved deep channels through the creative landscape. Yet from these fault lines emerged new growth – a period marked both by innovation born of necessity and by the lasting scars of austerity. Like roots breaking through stone, British designers adapted and flourished – their work becoming more intentional, more politically aware, more socially attuned.

These disruptions stretched beyond the political. Digital tools reshaped design, from artificial intelligence to algorithm-driven misinformation, creating ethical dilemmas even as they democratised creativity. Sustainability, once peripheral, became central, embedding itself into fashion, architecture and product design. Activism surged into digital spaces, where viral protest graphics and subversive branding challenged institutions in real time. Design was no longer just a reflection of change – it was the battleground on which these struggles played out.

Political and economic disruption shook the foundations of British design, forcing creative industries to navigate a landscape reshaped by austerity. The 2012 tuition fee increase placed new financial barriers on design and architecture education, pricing many students out of creative fields. Cuts to arts and cultural funding left institutions scrambling for private investment, while local authority budget reductions stalled public architecture projects and drained urban planning resources. The National Planning Policy Framework (2012) accelerated developer-led urbanism, expanding private sector influence over the built environment. Meanwhile Renzo Piano's The Shard (2012) pierced the skyline like a crystalline monolith of wealth, power and foreign capital, reflecting London's status as both a global financial hub and an isolated city of increasing inequality. For some, it symbolised prosperity; for others, it embodied the growing divide between those who benefited from economic recovery and those left behind.

Austerity sparked resistance across British society, from trade unions striking against public sector cuts to grassroots movements demanding economic justice. Unions like PCS led major industrial actions, while student protests erupted nationwide. The 2011 occupation of Hetherington House

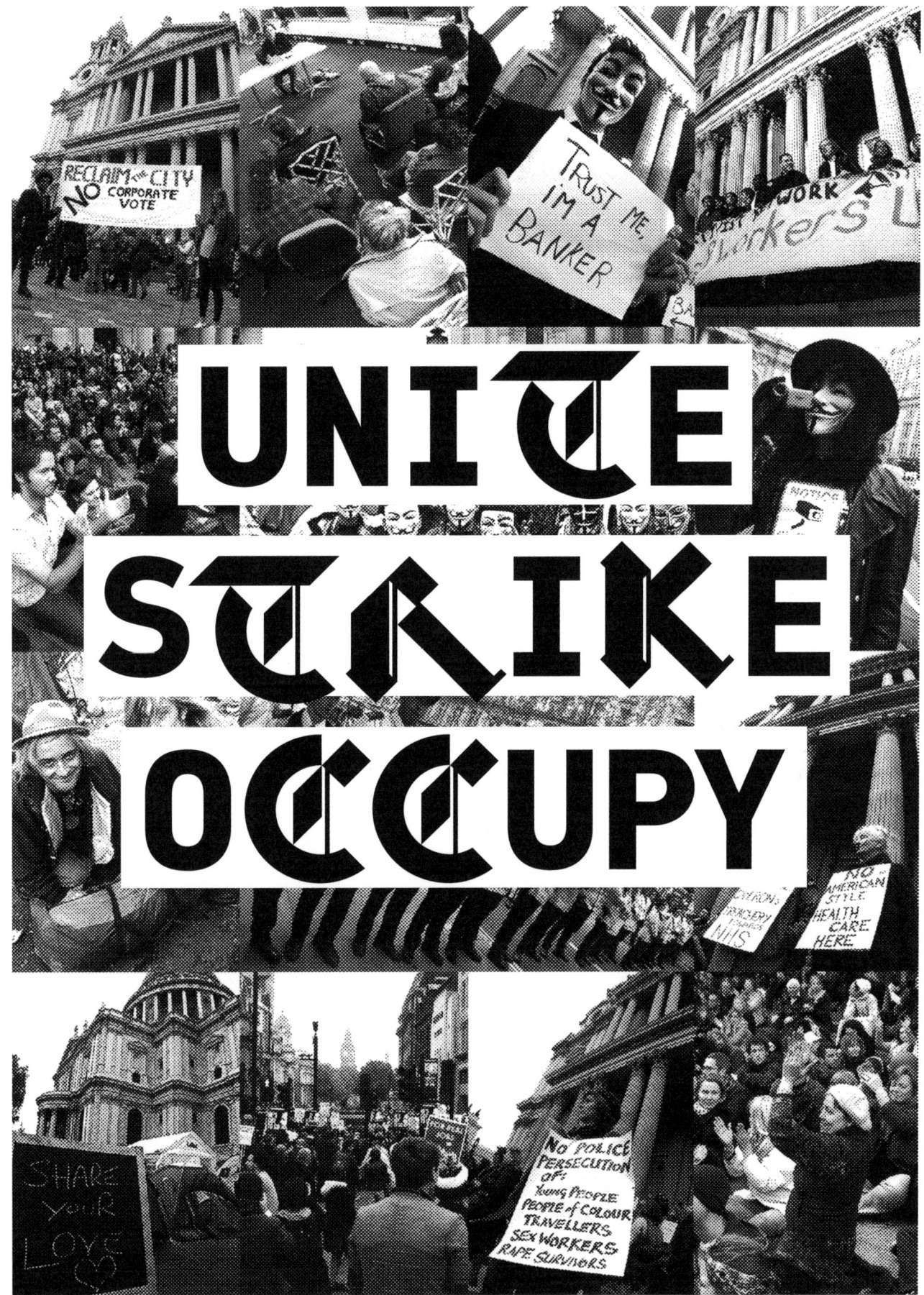

– one of the UK's longest-running student-led protests – became a defining stand against tuition hikes and education cuts. In architecture, the RIBA's 2019 training overhaul sought to make the profession more accessible, while the London School of Architecture introduced a cost-reducing model in 2015 that paired students with practices. Yet few visual responses to austerity were as striking as *The Occupied Times of London* (2011–16), born from the Occupy movement. Through radical graphics and activist publishing, it gave voice to a generation disillusioned with economic injustice. Austerity reshaped the landscape but also provoked a wave of creative resistance, proving that design was a tool not just of expression, but of defiance.

Amid the turbulence of austerity, the 2012 London Olympics offered a fleeting moment of national pride – one in which, as Cat Drew details in her introduction to this chapter, British design was celebrated on a global stage. Stella McCartney made history as the first fashion designer to create an Olympic kit, reimagining the Union Jack into a bold, modern motif for Team GB's apparel. Blending performance, aesthetics and sustainability, her designs set a new standard for national team uniforms. That same year, Thomas Heatherwick's New Routemaster bus, with its distinctive glass staircases and hop-on-hop-off platform, paid homage to London's heritage while embracing contemporary design. The Farrell Review (2014) reinforced this continuity, advocating for heritage-led regeneration and placemaking – ideas that would echo through the 2019 National Design Guide's vision for quality housing. Yet even as Britain celebrated its design legacy, fractures in its identity deepened.

By the middle of the decade, those fractures widened into the unthinkable. The 2016 Brexit referendum was more than a political decision: it was a rupture that reconfigured Britain's political, economic and cultural identity overnight. As its shadow lengthened across the creative landscape, design became central. The Vote Leave campaign's red bus, built on misinformation, demonstrated graphic design's raw emotional power, while Britain Stronger in Europe's campaign, although technically sound, struggled to match its visceral appeal. In the referendum's aftermath, British firms scrambled to maintain continental ties. Major architecture practices like Foster + Partners opened offices in European capitals, while smaller studios built networks to navigate barriers. Brexit deepened Britain's cultural divisions, influencing branding, advertising and consumer identity in polarised ways.

By the end of the decade, austerity and Brexit had fundamentally reshaped Britain's design ecosystem. The departure of European talent and persistent trade uncertainties created headwinds for manufacturing and product design. Yet these pressures also catalysed innovation, pushing practitioners towards deeper engagement with social issues and environmental activism. The decade's turbulence had fostered a more resilient, socially conscious design culture – one that didn't just weather storms but learned to dance in the rain.

Building on this spirit of adaptation and innovation, digital disruption rewired the infrastructure of British design, altering both practice and perception. In the private sector, innovation bloomed in unexpected places. Dyson disrupted its own market with the V10 cordless vacuum (2018), marking

LEFT — Vote Leave campaign bus, 2016. A key symbol of the Brexit referendum, this red bus carried the controversial claim that leaving the EU would free up £350 million a week for the NHS, becoming one of the most debated images of the campaign (top); North Design, Britain Stronger in Europe campaign identity, 2016. North Design's identity featured a bold typographic logo with the word 'IN' highlighted, symbolising support for the UK's continued EU membership (bottom)

PREVIOUS PAGE — *The Occupied Times of London*, Issue 6, 30 November 2011. Designed by Lazaros Kakoulidis and Tzortzis Rallis, the design of this activist-run newspaper incorporated Jonathan Barnbrook's Bastard typeface and PF Din Mono, with each issue featuring a signature back-page placard or slogan. It was nominated for the Design Museum's Design of the Year Award for Graphics in 2013

RIGHT ustwo, *Monument Valley*, 2014. An award-winning mobile game blending Escher-inspired architecture with atmospheric puzzle design that is renowned for its minimalist aesthetics and immersive, dreamlike environments

BELOW Renzo Piano, The Shard, London, 2012. Standing at 310 metres, The Shard is the tallest building in the UK, its glass-clad, tapering form designed to reflect the sky and city while setting a benchmark for sustainable high-rise architecture

the end of corded models and redefining home appliances. Citymapper (2011) transformed urban navigation, while Burberry led luxury retail into the digital age with live-streamed shows and seamless online–offline experiences. Mary Katrantzou revolutionised digital print in fashion, using technology to craft intricate, hyperrealistic textiles. The Raspberry Pi (2012) sought to democratise computing, becoming the UK's best-selling computer and making coding accessible worldwide, fostering a new generation of digital makers. *Monument Valley* (2014) emerged from Ustwo Games' London studio as a masterpiece of digital storytelling, proving that mobile games could be both commercially successful and architecturally sublime.

The 2010s also saw Augmented and Virtual Realities (AR and VR) transform digital storytelling. *Björk Digital* (2016) at Somerset House introduced audiences to immersive, VR-powered musical experiences, while UK firms like Blippar (founded in 2011) and the platform Aurasma (launched the same year) pioneered AR that redefined branding and interactive design. Meanwhile, vTime XR (2015) explored social engagement in virtual spaces, and Universal Everything used AR/VR to create cutting-edge digital art installations. Advances in augmented reality bridged the digital and physical worlds, reshaping how brands and creatives engaged audiences.

In the decade's final years, artificial intelligence emerged as both a tool and collaborator, sparking both excitement and concern. DeepMind, acquired by Google, pioneered AI breakthroughs that reshaped fields from science to automation, influencing design thinking in unexpected ways. At The Bartlett School of Architecture, researchers collaborated with Foster + Partners to explore AI-driven urban planning, using generative algorithms to optimise layouts and performance. Es Devlin's *Please Feed the Lions* (2018) exemplified human–AI collaboration, transforming public input into machine-generated poetry displayed in Trafalgar Square. As AI's creative potential expanded, it raised questions not just about automation, but about the evolving relationship between human intuition and machine intelligence.

By 2019, digital design had evolved from a specialised discipline into the fabric of British creativity. What began as a quest for better user experiences had become a dialogue about technology's role in society, ethics in design and the future of human–computer interaction. The digital revolution had not just changed how designers worked – it had fundamentally altered what it meant to be a designer in the modern world, demanding a new balance between innovation and responsibility.

As digital tools transformed design processes and ethics, another shift was under way – one that redefined not just how designers worked, but the very materials they worked with. Environmental disruption emerged as the most profound force of change, as sustainability moved from a peripheral concern to design's central pillar. The decade opened with pioneering innovations like the Plumen 001 lightbulb (2010), which won the Design Museum's Designs of the Year Award, proving that energy efficiency could dance gracefully with aesthetics. This breakthrough was followed by a wave of sustainable innovation across industries, demonstrating how ecological consciousness could drive

both creativity and commercial success. From Burberry's mid-decade elimination of plastic packaging to the growing push for sustainable textiles in luxury fashion, sustainability affected every aspect of design thinking.

By mid-decade, as public awareness of climate change intensified and regulations tightened, sustainability deepened its roots, branching into speculative design and systems thinking. Foster + Partners led the charge with two landmark projects: Bloomberg HQ (2017) in London, the highest-rated BREEAM office at the time, and Apple Park in California (2017), showcasing British architectural innovation on a global scale. In one of the decade's most significant moments for British design, John Pawson's reimagining of the Commonwealth Institute into the new Design Museum (2016) demonstrated how creative reuse could honour both heritage and sustainability. These were not just buildings – they were manifestos in glass and steel, declaring that sustainability and sophistication could coexist.

As the decade drew to a close, a new wave of visionaries redefined sustainable British fashion. Against a backdrop of growing fascination with Mars exploration, Christopher Raeburn's SS20 New Horizons collection captured this zeitgeist, imagining clothing for future Mars inhabitants while transforming military surplus into sustainable fashion. Alongside Raeburn, designers like Bethany Williams and Helen Kirkum gained recognition for their innovative approaches to circular fashion and zero-waste design. What began as material innovation had become a paradigm shift, reconfiguring how British designers approached their craft.

As environmental consciousness grew, so too did social activism. The 2010s erupted in a cascade of disruptive

BELOW — RÆBURN, Spring/Summer 2020 New Horizons collection. Debuted in 2019, this collection explores sustainable fashion by repurposing materials like parachutes and solar blankets, drawing inspiration from the challenges of living on Mars to rethink our approach to making, living and consuming (left); JW Anderson, Autumn/Winter 2013 Menswear collection. Anderson's collection challenged traditional menswear norms by incorporating elements such as short culottes, flamenco-inspired frills and strapless tops, exploring themes of gender fluidity and androgyny (right)

PREVIOUS SPREAD — Es Devlin, *Please Feed the Lions*, London Design Festival, Trafalgar Square, 2018. This interactive installation used AI to transform public contributions into generative poetry, which was then projected onto Nelson's Column, demonstrating AI's role in creative expression

LEFT — Foster + Partners, Apple Park, Cupertino, 2017. Apple's headquarters is a vast, ring-shaped campus designed to blend high-tech innovation with sustainability, featuring a seamless glass façade, extensive green spaces and one of the world's largest naturally ventilated buildings

RIGHT — John Pawson, the Design Museum, London, 2016. Housed in the former Commonwealth Institute, the Design Museum's new home preserves its iconic hyperbolic paraboloid roof while introducing a minimalist interior, creating a contemporary space for exhibitions and public programmes

protest, from Occupy to the Arab Spring, unfolding in an entirely new visual and digital landscape. Unlike the bold screen-printed posters of the 1960s and '70s, contemporary activism was shaped by viral social media campaigns, open-source graphic systems and instant digital dissemination. Protest design was no longer confined to placards and print – it lived on Instagram grids, Twitter feeds and TikTok loops, evolving in real time with political currents. As 'woke' consciousness spread online, design became an ever more inclusive yet politically charged medium.

This activist spirit also flowed through fashion, where JW Anderson's gender-neutral designs of 2013 dissolved traditional binaries, perhaps channelling David Bowie's boundary-breaking legacy. Jonathan Barnbrook's *Blackstar* (2016) album cover for Bowie's final release, unveiled just days before his death, was a crystallisation of Bowie's haunting meditation on mortality and identity, weaving together threads of gender fluidity and artistic rebellion. British fashion houses embraced broader strokes of multi-culturalism and inclusivity, while Daniel W. Fletcher emerged as a powerful voice in political fashion – his collections composing eloquent commentary on British identity in Brexit's shadow.

Design's role in protest movements found powerful expression through platforms like *gal-dem* (2015–22), which orchestrated a symphony of under-represented voices in British media and design. Extinction Rebellion's stark visual identity (2018) and the Justice4Grenfell campaign's Three Billboards Protest (2018) exemplified how design could demand accountability and drive change. Led By Donkeys (founded in 2018) weaponised billboard advertising, exposing politicians' contradictory statements through large-scale installations that spread virally across social media. By decade's end, British design was inseparable from identity politics and digital activism – one retweet, share and story at a time.

The 2010s marked a seismic shift in British design's evolution, transforming it from a discipline once defined by form and function into a powerful force for social change, environmental stewardship and technological innovation. Designers didn't just respond to disruption – they redefined their roles within it, weaving sustainability, digital innovation and social consciousness into the very fabric of their work.

The decade's legacy lives on in multiple dimensions. Austerity and Brexit forced designers to rethink how they worked, while digital innovation and artificial intelligence redefined not just creative practice but also how society engaged with design. Sustainability, once an afterthought, became a necessity, and design activism found renewed urgency. As the next decade unfolds, these pressures will only intensify. The challenges of climate change, automation and inequality will continue to shape British design in ways we cannot yet fully predict. Yet if the 2010s proved anything, it is that designers do not merely react to change – they shape it. The turbulence of the decade didn't just challenge them; it reshaped them, forging a generation acutely aware of design's role in an unstable world of fake news and alternative facts. Their greatest task is no longer just about technical mastery or the refinement of taste, but about the ability to imagine – and fight for – better worlds.

TOP Led By Donkeys, anti-Brexit billboard featuring Nigel Farage, Edinburgh, April 2019. This billboard displayed a past statement by Nigel Farage, highlighting perceived contradictions in his stance on Brexit

BOTTOM Jonathan Barnbrook, Occupy London logo, 2012. Chosen through a public vote, Barnbrook's design replaced an earlier roundel-based symbol, using the initials 'O' and 'L' to represent location and movement, aligning with the decentralised nature of Occupy London

OPPOSITE Extinction Rebellion protest, London Fashion Week, The Strand, 17 September 2019. This high-profile demonstration against the fashion industry's environmental impact featured protesters carrying banners and flags with the group's hourglass logo – a symbol of time running out for Earth's species (top); Justice4Grenfell and BBH Labs, Three Billboards Outside Grenfell protest, 2018. Inspired by the film *Three Billboards Outside Ebbing, Missouri*, this campaign used stark red billboards with bold black text to highlight the lack of justice and accountability following the Grenfell Tower fire (bottom)

LIBERTY.

OPPOSITE Tresco, early 2010s

Tresco
Watercolour Florals for a Digital Age

Tresco is a vibrant watercolour study celebrating an exquisite array of plant species from around the world. This hand-painted design draws inspiration from the diverse flora of Tresco Abbey Garden on the Isles of Scilly, featuring flowers, ferns and succulents from its windswept sand dunes and carefully landscaped borders.

In the early 2010s, the advent of digital textile-printing technology marked a turning point for the industry, offering unprecedented creative possibilities. Unlike traditional methods – limited in colour, scale and detail – digital printing enabled high-resolution, photorealistic reproductions that captured even the subtlest nuances of an original artwork. For Liberty, this technology provided freedom to explore customisation, scale and colour in ways previously unattainable. Designers could now incorporate intricate textures, gradients and vibrant hues directly onto fabric, greatly expanding artistic expression. Watercolour designs like Tresco could finally be reproduced with the full depth, transparency and fluidity of the original brushstrokes. This innovation allowed Liberty to push its creative boundaries and set a new standard for textile artistry.

The 2020s

Designing Our Future

Design for Planet: The Design Council's Vision for a Regenerative World
Minnie Moll

Tectonic shifts

The early 2020s have been defined by global challenges, from the COVID-19 pandemic to geopolitical conflicts and economic pressures. The most pressing of these is the climate emergency. Extreme weather events, biodiversity loss and environmental degradation are unfolding faster than many predicted. Our consumer economy is depleting natural resources more rapidly than they can be replenished, demanding a fundamental redesign of how we live. Given that eighty per cent of a product's environmental impact is determined at the design stage, we must design differently. We need to redesign how we design.

The Design Council was created in 1944 (as the Council of Industrial Design) to help shape a post-war consumer economy. Now, eighty years later, the Council's role must shift to helping our consumer economy to make the transition into a regenerative society. With a climate time bomb ticking and options running out. Designers have immense power to drive the change we need to see, and with that power comes responsibility.

A new responsibility: Design for Planet

In 2021, the Design Council conducted a strategic review, which led to a single mission: Design for Planet. Alongside this, a new long-term vision was established, aiming to create a regenerative world for all.

It was a bold decision from the Board of Trustees, chaired by Terry Tyrrell, to support this singular mission and galvanise the nearly two million designers in the UK to place planetary needs at the forefront of their work.

When COP26 took place in Glasgow in November 2021, the Council accelerated its plans to be part of that moment. It was, in effect, building the plane while flying, seeking input along the way. Confidence in this direction increased when the Council's Chief Design Officer, Cat Drew, and I met up with the influential economist Kate Raworth, author of *Doughnut Economics*. Raworth's question – 'If you're not designing for planet, what planet are you on?' – became a rallying cry for the Council's mission.

OPPOSITE Design Council, Design for Planet visual identity, 2023

PREVIOUS PAGE Grimshaw, Maynard, Equation and AtkinsRéalis, Elizabeth Line, 2022. Commissioned by Crossrail, the Elizabeth Line is one of London's most significant infrastructure projects, spanning 62 miles with 10 new stations and carrying 200 million passengers annually. Its cohesive design language and focus on accessibility reinforce the value of public investment in architecture and design, earning it the RIBA Stirling Prize in 2024

The language was intentionally chosen to include the climate and *all* life on our precious planet, not just humanity. It underscores reducing emissions, promoting biodiversity and achieving a 'nature-positive' future. Without biodiversity, our ecosystems and ultimately human life are at risk.

Design for Planet aspires to be a movement, a call to action for the design community. It represents a new definition of good design, and an evolution from the Council's founding focus on aesthetics and functional value to a more inclusive and planet-centric approach.

Design for Planet in action

The Design for Planet mission embraces themes such as circular economy, whole-system change and designing with nature. It focuses on materials, modularity and repairability. It draws attention, too, to what we design in and what we design out – such as waste. A great example of this in action is the work of Morrama Ltd, whose Kibu Circular Headphones for children can be taken apart and repaired to minimise waste. We also have to design for mitigation and adaptation.

Innovations in sustainable materials, from cling film made of fish scales to architectural applications of mycelium, are exciting developments. However, scaling these innovations and securing investment remain critical next steps. Technology, including AI, plays a role in expanding the impact of design. AI is already having a transformative role in architecture, revolutionising how we can analyse data to design for energy efficiency.

Several organisations have pioneered sustainable design for years, including the UK Green Building Council and the Ellen MacArthur Foundation. More recent initiatives – such as the Future Observatory partnership between the Arts and Humanities Research Council (AHRC) and the Design Museum, and the British Fashion Council's Institute of Positive Fashion – are contributing to the wider movement.

Central to the Design Council's efforts has been its annual Design for Planet Festival, which was launched in 2021 at the V&A Dundee in support of COP26.

ABOVE   Future Observatory, visual identity by SPIN, 2021. The Design Museum's national research programme explores how design can address climate change (top); Morrama Ltd, Kibu Circular Headphones, 2024 (bottom)

LEFT   Design Council, Systemic Design Framework, 2023

ABOVE Design Council staff at the first annual Design for Planet Festival, V&A Dundee, 2021

Subsequent editions took place at Northumbria University; the University of East Anglia; and, in 2024, Manchester MET School of Art. This event brings together designers, businesses and government institutions to share knowledge. With more than 20,000 combined global attendees, it has become a vital platform for exchanging ideas and inspiration.

Featured thought leaders – including Sophie Thomas (sustainable and circular design), Michael Pawlyn (regenerative design and biomimicry) and Indy Johar (architecture and sustainable urbanisation) – have long championed sustainability principles, waiting for the rest of us to catch up. They, along with many other Festival contributors, have been especially provocative about how design must evolve, emphasising the need for shared use, durable products, a return to resourceful pre-industrial methods and 'cathedral thinking' that fosters long stewardship. They also call for a new generation of 'menders, repairers, fixers and hackers', and argue that designers should aspire to be 'waste entrepreneurs' or 'contemporary alchemists', capable of transforming discarded materials into valuable resources.

There is a call for greater humility in design, too. As Dr Simone Ferracina from the University of Edinburgh stated at the 2022 Design for Planet Festival, 'Designers must care more about people and about what exists already, and about the planet, than about the expression of their own creativity or intentions or ideas'. Now that throws down a real challenge for many designers.

In 2021, the Design Council launched the Systemic Design Framework, an evolution of the Double Diamond model. It expands the model to encompass the importance of stakeholder engagement and the 'invisible activities' that sit around the design process, addressing the interconnected nature of design challenges and fostering a mindset and methodology suitable for systemic change. The twentieth anniversary of the Double Diamond was marked in 2023 at an event, hosted by IDEO, celebrating a milestone in design thinking. The tool was registered under a Creative Commons licence, making it freely accessible to designers who can adapt it as needed.

To measure the impact of design, the Design Value Framework was introduced, assessing the social, democratic, financial and environmental value created by design. This approach empowers designers to place sustainability at the heart of their work.

The Council's 'Green Design Skills Gap Report' of 2024 highlighted the urgent need to equip designers with green design skills at every level. In response, an ambitious goal was set to upskill one million designers in green design by 2030, from the classroom to the C-Suite. Working with education partners and the wider design community, the Council is currently co-designing a programme to achieve this bold ambition.

Also in 2024, the 'Blueprint for Renewal: Design and Technology Education' was launched in partnership with key stakeholders, offering policy recommendations to government on a critical review of GCSE Design & Technology to address the 67 per cent drop seen in young people taking the qualification over the last ten years.

That autumn, the Design Council established the Homes Taskforce – a cohort of eight design leaders including Sadie Morgan, Sunand Prasad and Hanif Kara – offering support to the newly elected government in delivering 1.5 million homes within UK climate commitments.

Powerful together

Design for Planet's achievements so far are owed to widespread support from the design community, including nearly 250 Design Council Experts bringing a breadth of sustainable design experience.

The Council is proud to work in partnership with UK Research and Innovation (UKRI) and its constituent councils, AHRC and Innovate UK, alongside numerous private and public partners. These partnerships have included major infrastructure bodies such as Network Rail, Homes England, National Highways and Anglian Water.

In 2025, the Design Council will host the World Design Organization's biannual World Design Congress™ at the Barbican Centre in London, uniting the

OPPOSITE World Design Congress Ambassadors at the Barbican Centre, 2025. From left to right: fashion designer Foday Dumbuya; artist and stage designer Es Devlin; creative and technology leader Suhair Khan; industrial designer Tom Dixon; and architect and writer Prof Lesley Lokko OBE. These five prominent figures champion the Design for Planet mission, leading up to the World Design Congress 2025

BELOW Design Council, Design Value Framework, 2023

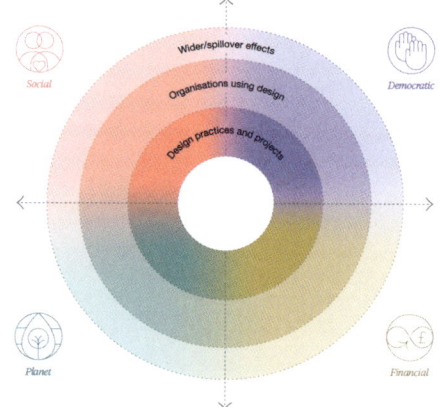

LEFT Roundtable of the Design Council Homes Task Force, Westminster, London, October 2024. From left to right: Summer Islam, Peter Maxwell, Ruth Lang, Gideon Amos MP, Emily Darlington MP, Phineas Harper, Graham Thomas, Yemi Aladerun, Sadie Morgan OBE, Peter Lamb MP, Roger Madelin, Louise Whyman, George Clarke, Deborah Nagan, Astrid Smitham, Edward Hobson, Claire Bennie, Yolande Barnes, Kathryn Firth

global design community to accelerate action on climate change. This event will amplify the Design for Planet message and spark collective efforts towards a regenerative future. If there has ever been a time to strengthen the global design community, it is now.

A bright future for design

Design currently contributes nearly £100 billion to the UK economy and is an integral part of the creative industries, one of the government's priority growth sectors. Design can be a transformative asset in creating green skills, green jobs and a green economy.

Although a regenerative world for all remains a distant vision, it is clear that good design is indispensable to achieving it – good design being design that works in harmony with nature instead of against it, in order to achieve net zero and nature positive.

The task ahead is to engage the design sector, commissioners of design, government and the public in recognising and harnessing the full potential of design, thereby accelerating the critical transition needed. There is no time to lose.

Design has achieved extraordinary things over the last eighty years, and the Design Council will continue to champion, convene and catalyse action throughout the 2020s and beyond.

A Decade of Reckoning: Design at a Turning Point
Priya Khanchandani

The 2020s has been relentless – a decade we are barely halfway through, yet one that is already defined by a radical reshaping of our world. It began with Brexit, which saw Britain depart from the European Union on 31 January 2020, leading the country into a period of instability as the economy began to suffer. Productivity slowed, and the end of free movement disrupted British industries in ways that many had underestimated, impacting 'us' more than it affected 'them'. Then came COVID-19, which hit the UK at around the same time, triggering from March a series of lockdowns to curb the spread of the pandemic. These measures forced a profound shift in how we live, shaking us into a new understanding of our health and mortality.

As the pandemic exposed the fragility of global systems, another crisis erupted – one that forced a reckoning with racial injustice and colonial legacies. In May 2020, the police officer Derek Chauvin knelt on the neck of George Floyd and suffocated him to death, sparking waves of protests at the site of the crime in Minneapolis, as well as across the US and in more than fifty countries around the world, including the UK. That June, the protests reached Bristol, a city steeped in British colonial history, where a statue celebrating the seventeenth-century slave trader Edward Colston was toppled, dragged to the harbour and defiantly thrown into the water. These events would shake the status quo everywhere. In Britain, they would not only change the face of culture, but also tug at the conventional definitions of Britishness. Working at the Design Museum, I watched and felt the significance of design shifting beneath my feet as designers evolved and the discipline showed itself to be capable of helping us adapt and be responsive to change.

During the pandemic, design defied its stereotype of being purely about frivolous styling, emerging instead as a powerful tool for protecting lives. The sheer will behind small-scale initiatives driven by fashion brands, for example, helped them to bypass the bureaucracy that had been preventing personal protective equipment (PPE) from becoming available through official channels. Phoebe English, Holly Fulton, Cozette McCreary and Bethany Williams joined forces to form the Emergency Designer Network (EDN) in March 2020, after Fulton was contacted by hospitals and hospices about supplying them with PPE. They managed to create a workable product by cutting a pattern from scrubs provided by the Royal Free Hospital and sourcing fabric from an NHS supplier; we displayed this at the Design Museum as part of *Bethany Williams: Alternative Systems* – an exhibition that included a section about the EDN. Meanwhile, on an industrial scale, the aerospace and automotive industries combined their efforts to support the manufacture of ventilators. A group involving Rolls-Royce, Airbus and BAE Systems, as well as Ford and McLaren, helped ramp up production by the UK ventilator manufacturers Penlon and Smiths Group, allowing seven new factories to be built in a matter of weeks. The adaptability and speed of solutions generated thanks to the inventiveness of design was uplifting.

Design quickly became more relevant in everyday life, too. As the tangible world faded into the background and – with the exception of essential workers – so many of us

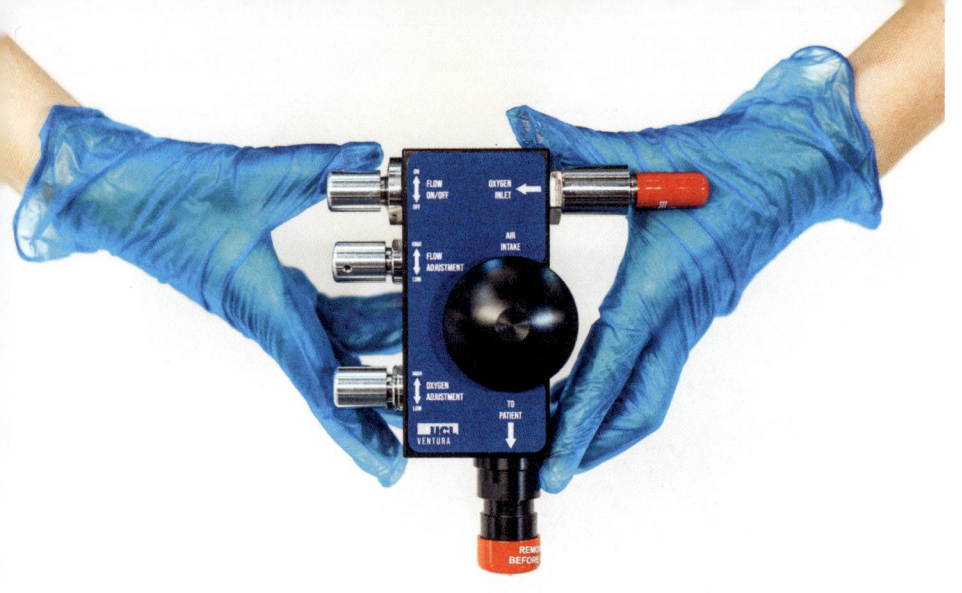

LEFT — Mercedes-AMG HPP and UCL, UCL-Ventura breathing aid, 2020. Developed in under 100 hours, this non-invasive device helped COVID-19 patients breathe more easily and reduced the need for ventilators in intensive care units. Its design was made freely available worldwide, allowing manufacturers across the globe to produce it at scale

PREVIOUS SPREAD — Banksy, Brexit mural, Dover, 2017. Depicting a worker chiselling a star from the EU flag, this political artwork anticipated the UK's departure from the European Union, which became official in early 2020

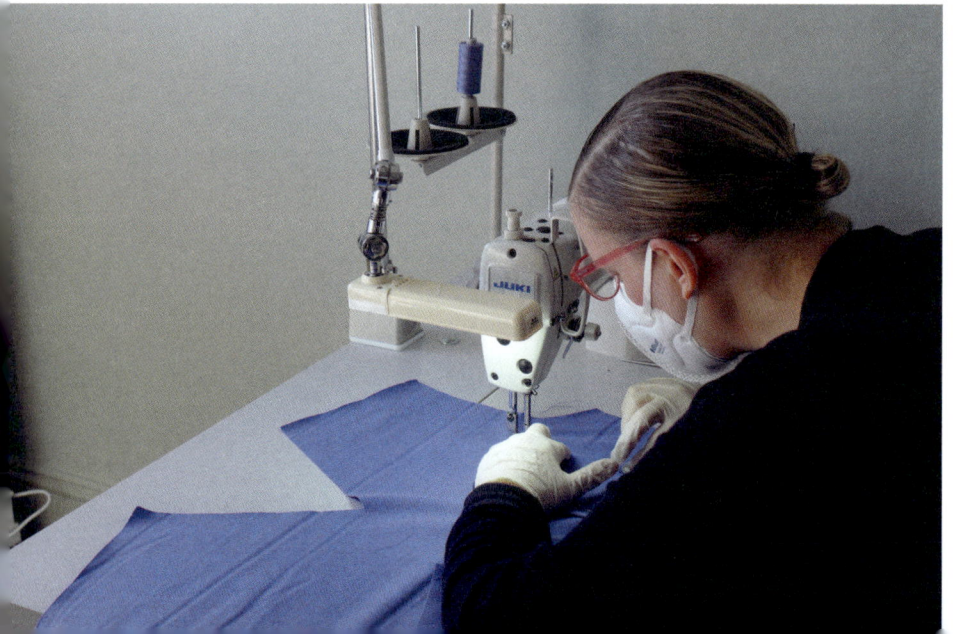

MIDDLE — Black Lives Matter protest, London, 3 June 2020. Protesters march through the streets following a gathering in Hyde Park, where thousands, including actor John Boyega, demonstrated against the death of George Floyd before moving through central London past landmarks such as Parliament Square and Downing Street

LEFT — Emergency Designer Network (EDN), 2020. A volunteer-led initiative that rapidly mobilised designers and manufacturers to produce scrubs and other essential garments for NHS hospital staff during the COVID-19 pandemic

became confined mostly to our homes, we were forced to migrate our lives online. The endless portals and boundless pages of the internet were supposed to liberate us, providing a democratised realm for social interactions, but those of us working in white-collar settings found our interactions shifting online in a way that became disconcerting. In a column for *Frieze* magazine in 2020, I reflected on our increased awareness of our digital self-image, which I described as a new stage of self-representation following on from the 'mirror stage' of Lacanian psychoanalysis. Heightened by the increased proliferation of WhatsApp and social media more broadly, contemplating the world online shifted our conception of who we are. We created carefully designed profiles and top-half-only outfits, and sought to replicate the real world through the intangibility and screen-wide shape of the digital world. For many, this was a way of creating connection in the absence of physical interaction with others; for designers, it meant adapting their aesthetics to 'screen-first' identities, with those who had a strong digital presence emerging as major cultural voices.

The home became the epicentre of our lives, and design took on new significance as a medium for self-expression and creativity. Yes, there were beige living rooms, but there were also effusive expressions of hand-painted colour and resourceful IKEA hacks. Our relationship with technology and domesticity, the interplay between the intangible and the tangible, were at once all up in the air, and it would take several years before we knew where things would land in a new reality that is ever-evolving. As AI advances in healthcare, finance and transport, it remains to be seen how the design process will be further reshaped by technology, but we are already seeing image generators such as DALL-E, Stable Diffusion and Midjourney create fantasy worlds – and start to make strides as tools for designing buildings and products.

The George Floyd protests were a wake-up call across the UK cultural industries – including the design sector – that they had been exclusionary of Black voices and of POC more broadly. There was scepticism about actions such as black squares on Instagram, on the grounds that they only paid lip service to the serious issues at hand. But the spaces where transformation did occur sparked shock waves. When Counterspace, headed by South African architect Sumayya Vally, designed the Serpentine Pavilion in 2021, it moved me with its enigmatically arranged architectural fragments, its careful use of scale and light, and the way it gave voice to diasporic communities. I'll also never forget the 2022 exhibition *Body Vessel Clay* at Two Temple Place, which celebrated ceramics made by Black women. The materiality of the voluminous pots, asymmetric forms, stoneware plates and vases brought together by curator Jareh Das offered a powerful and yet under-represented world view.

In May 2023, the eighteenth edition of the Venice Architecture Biennale launched under the curatorship of the Scottish–Ghanaian architect and educator Lesley Lokko. The first curator of African origin and also the first to spotlight Africa and its diaspora at Venice, Lokko had studied at The Bartlett School of Architecture at UCL before founding the Graduate School of Architecture at the University of Johannesburg and setting up the African Futures Institute. She had recently left a role as Dean of the Spitzer School of Architecture at City College of New York on the basis of its

RIGHT Black Lives Matter protest sign, London, 2020. A powerful example of graphic design in activism, this redrawn Black Lives Matter logo and lettering – modeled on the movement's official flag – reflect its grassroots energy. As a globally recognised symbol of resistance and solidarity, it has been prominently displayed in protests against racial injustice and police violence

structural resistance to change in an act that she described at the time as 'self-preservation'. Her Biennale radically challenged the Western construction of architecture and was a refreshing example of how to move forward with pluralistic framings of design. I happened to be at the Royal Institute of British Architects when the letters of Lokko's name were being intricately hand-painted on to the wall after she was awarded the 2024 Royal Gold Medal for Architecture, acknowledging her dedication to democratising architecture and promoting diverse perspectives within the discipline.

During the month that the Venice Biennale launched, *The Offbeat Sari* opened at the Design Museum, an exhibition and book I'd been developing for some years about the significance of the sari in contemporary India. It explored the sari as an object in transition in terms of design, as a vessel for the expression of plural identities and as a mode of dress under evolution through experimentation with craft. Staging an exhibition dedicated to South Asia was a first in the Design Museum's history, and it felt momentous since South Asia is a place that had long been misunderstood, partly because it is often perceived as being defined by its colonial past. Curating *The Offbeat Sari* was an opportunity to showcase the work of many incredible contemporary designers whose creations are little known internationally. Around the same time, we held a display about the work of London-based designer Yinka Ilori, whose practice had designed the 2019 Dulwich Pavilion *Colour Palace* with Pricegore architects, and begun to grow exponentially since then. His work, reflecting his Nigerian–British dual heritage, brought the museum's atrium to life with colour and pattern. Holding these two exhibitions concurrently felt powerful.

For the first time in my career, the voices and perspectives of contemporary diasporic designers in London were dominating the mainstream.

Also in 2023, engineer Hanif Kara was awarded the London Design Medal, the highest accolade for an individual who has contributed to the design industry, and the other medals went to architect and entrepreneur Pooja Agrawal, POoR Collective and ceramicist Magdalene Odundo. Kara, the Design Director and co-founder of AKT II, was born in Uganda and moved to the UK in the 1970s as a refugee. He worked at a car manufacturer and as a draughtsman, before landing a place at the University of Salford to study engineering. In a success story that it feels important to acknowledge at a time when the value of immigration is being tested, his practice has now won more than 350 design awards, including serving as structural engineers for the RIBA Stirling Prize-winning Peckham Library in 2000, and he was awarded an OBE for his services to architecture, engineering and education in the 2022 New Year Honours List.

After decades of unchecked consumerism, the design industry has experienced a further reckoning. Sustainability is no longer an abstract idea but an urgent necessity, driven by the undeniable realities of climate change. From the wildfires devastating California to the record-breaking heatwaves across Europe, the environmental crisis has forced designers to recognise the importance of their role in shaping a more responsible future. The Design Council's new mission Design for Planet highlights the essential state-sponsored effort to bolster sustainable design and the transition to a green economy, while the drive towards

LEFT	Mikhail Riches, Goldsmith Street, Norwich, 2019. The only social housing scheme to win the Stirling Prize, it set a new standard for sustainable design
ABOVE	Brazilian Pavilion, Terra, Venice Architecture Biennale, 2023. The Biennale awarded Brazil the Golden Lion for its exploration of Indigenous land rights, environmental justice and decolonisation
OPPOSITE	Sumayya Vally, Counterspace, Serpentine Pavilion, 2021

a net-zero economy has been incorporated into corporate strategies across architecture, fashion and design. With affordable, eco-friendly products becoming a market glut and energy-guzzling design fairs continuing to grow across the world, sustainability could be described as soft capitalism. The coming years will determine how this movement creates real systemic change.

There are designers who have started to break the mould. Designer Natsai Audrey Chieza of Faber Futures, for example, is working to develop a vision for bio-based products that can bring about a biophilic culture to act on the climate crisis, through products such as a jacket made with microbial dye and prints made using algae-derived black pigment. Born in Zimbabwe, she studied architecture in Edinburgh and set up her studio in London before moving to Oslo. Based in London, James Shaw started working with waste as a student and has established a design practice that takes discarded objects, mainly made from plastic, and deconstructs them to turn them into desirable objects and sculptures like a drinks trolley, a planter and a set of shelves. A whole community of designers – Superflux, Cooking Sections, Iris van Herpen and Stella McCartney – are working at the cutting edge of an exploratory design that is friendlier to the planet.

As designers rethink materiality and consumption, architects are also embracing a new consciousness – one that prioritises resilience and a deeper connection to the environments we inhabit. Designed by Mikhail Riches, Goldsmith Street is the only social housing scheme to have won the Stirling Prize, awarded annually to the UK's best new building. Comprising 105 homes, arranged into high-density terraces close to Norwich city centre, it is the largest development of its kind built to the Passivhaus standard, achieving energy bills that are 70 per cent lower than the average household in the UK. The way architects use materials is evolving, too. Engineer Steve Webb, Pierre Bidaud of the Rutland-based Stonemasonry Company and London-based architect Amin Taha collaborated to employ stone to build a residential tower on Finchley Road, north London, on the basis that it is as durable as steel and concrete but much more sustainable because it is extracted in a manner that consumes far less energy.

From global crises to cultural shifts, the 2020s has been far from plain sailing – so much so that there is the sense we have been catapulted through half a century rather than half a decade. In recent years, design has proven itself to be not just a reflection of change but also a force that shapes change. The new voices now starting to lead the conversation, the digital realms redefining identity and the push for sustainability that is starting to emerge signal that design is no longer just about aesthetics – it is also about survival, identity and justice. Yet, as we navigate an era of conflict, climate emergency and rapid technological transformation, the question remains as to whether design will challenge the status quo or be co-opted by the very systems it seeks to disrupt. The coming years will determine whether this moment marks the birth of a more inclusive, conscious and resilient design future – or is just another fleeting trend. Those of us hungry to pave the way to the future know which side of design history we would like to be on.

RIGHT — *Yinka Ilori: Parables for Happiness* exhibition, the Design Museum, 2022. Celebrating Ilori's distinctive use of colour and pattern, this exhibition explored his multidisciplinary approach to design, drawing on storytelling and cultural heritage to create joyful, immersive spaces

OPPOSITE — James Shaw, *Strange Friends*, Hauser & Wirth Mayfair, 2023. A series of objects showcasing Shaw's experimental use of recycled materials and sustainable making techniques (top); *The Offbeat Sari* exhibition, the Design Museum, 2023. Exploring the contemporary reinvention of the sari in India and beyond, this exhibition showcased its evolution from a traditional garment to a dynamic expression of identity, fashion and activism (bottom)

PREVIOUS SPREAD — Faber Futures and Ginkgo Bioworks, Normal Phenomena of Life (NPOL) campaign, 2023. Co-founded by Natsai Audrey Chieza, NPOL explores sustainable textile innovations, including the Exploring Jacket, a silk garment dyed with bacteria to reduce water use

188

LIBERTY.

OPPOSITE Lines Ballet, FuturLiberty 2023, curated by Federico Forquet, and Soho, 2020

Lines Ballet & Soho
Tradition Meets Digital Innovation

Created for the FuturLiberty fabrics capsule collection, curated by couturier and interior designer Federico Forquet and designed with Adam Herbert and Genevieve Bennett, Lines Ballet depicts an aerial view of a geometric landscape. Freshly ploughed fields are juxtaposed with bold, graphic shapes to create a playful print where clean lines jostle for attention. Meanwhile, Soho, from the Autumn/Winter 2020 collection, reinterprets a classic Tree of Life design, inspired by neon artistry and pure imagination. Hand-drawn in the Liberty design studio using fineliner pens and brought to life with vibrant gouache, Soho features arrows, light bulbs, mushrooms, hearts and flowers – all intertwined in a dazzling display.

Looking to the future while drawing from its rich heritage, the defining designs of the 2020s honour the creative vision of Polly Mason, Head of Design, and the pioneering influence of Mary-Ann Dunkley, Design Director. Through innovative collaborations, emerging trends and fresh talent, Liberty Fabrics has achieved new heights of international recognition. The company continues to challenge traditional aesthetics with imaginative interpretations, propelling the brand forward.

Pattern and Purpose: Liberty × Design Council Print Collaboration

Liberty has partnered with the Design Council to create a captivating series of prints inspired by the Council's refreshed Design for Planet and World Design Congress 2025 identity. Drawing from Hans Schleger's iconic eye-and-arrow logo, alongside the bold geometry of Brutalism and the distinctive architecture of the Barbican Centre, Liberty's creative team delved into its archives to uncover patterns that reflect a dynamic interplay of influences.

These designs seamlessly merge mid-century modernism's stylised silhouettes with trompe l'oeil geometrics, patchwork and camouflage-inspired motifs, celebrating both graphic precision and organic forms while perfectly capturing the essence of the Design for Planet ethos. The collaboration reimagines Liberty's archival artworks through a contemporary lens, uniting bold visual elements with naturalistic motifs to embody innovation and inspire a commitment to sustainability. The result is a timeless aesthetic that balances progress with an enduring respect for the environment.

RIGHT Linear Leaf (top) and Autumn Grove (bottom), The Liberty Design Studio, 2025

Biographies

Christopher Breward is Director of National Museums Scotland. He was previously Director of Collections and Research at the National Galleries of Scotland, Principal of Edinburgh College of Art at the University of Edinburgh, and Head of Research at the Victoria and Albert Museum. He has published widely on the histories of fashion, masculinity and urban cultures. His books include *Fashioning London* (2004), *The Suit: Form, Function and Style* (2016), and *British Design from 1948: Innovation in the Modern Age* (2012), which he co-edited. The exhibitions he has curated include *21st Century Dandy* (2002) with the British Council, *The London Look: Fashion from Street to Catwalk* (2004) at the Museum of London and *Sixties Fashion* (2006) at the Victoria and Albert Museum.

Cat Drew is Chief Design Officer at the Design Council, where she leads the Design for Planet mission to increase regenerative design skills and knowledge. She co-founded the UK Government's Policy Lab, pioneering the use of design in policymaking, and has held leadership roles at Uscreates and FutureGov, making public services more user-centred and systemic. She introduced speculative design to government policymaking, applying it for the first time in the UK to projects on ageing and rail, and led a major public engagement initiative to create the world's first Government AI & Data Ethics Framework. She is a member of design collective The Point People, a faculty member for States of Change, and sits on advisory boards for the Institute of Coding and the D&AD Impact Council. A recognised expert in systemic design, she frequently speaks on design's role in social innovation, and in 2019, she was inducted into the Design Week Hall of Fame.

Mark Cortes Favis is an editor, writer and graphic designer with expertise in design and architecture publishing. He has worked as an editor for leading cultural and academic institutions, including the Design Council, the Jencks Foundation at the Cosmic House, and The Bartlett School of Architecture, UCL. In 2015, he established and led the publishing department at the Design Museum, overseeing more than forty books on design and architecture. His edited books include *Designs of Our Time: 10 Years of Designs of the Year* (2019) and *The Design Museum in a Box* (2016), while his published titles include *California: Designing Freedom* (2017), *Waste Age: What Can Design Do?* (2021) and *Ai Weiwei: Making Sense* (2023). In addition to his editorial work, he has developed commercially driven publishing strategies, combining high-quality scholarship with innovative editorial design.

Max Fraser is a design commentator working across digital media, books, magazines, exhibitions, video and events to broaden the conversation around contemporary design and architecture. He is the author of multiple design books, including *Design UK* (2001) and *Designers on Design* (2004), co-written with Sir Terence Conran, as well as the London Design Guide series and monographs on Piet Hein Eek, Luca Nichetto and Benjamin Hubert. As a journalist, he has worked as a design correspondent for *CNN Style* and has written for publications including the *Financial Times*, *Wallpaper*, *Icon*, *Surface*, *London's Evening Standard* and *Newsweek International*. He has consulted for companies and organisations worldwide and was Deputy Director of the London Design Festival from 2012 to 2015. In 2023, he joined Dezeen as Editorial Director, having previously collaborated with the platform by co-publishing *Dezeen Book of Ideas* (2011), instigating the Brexit Design Manifesto with founder Marcus Fairs (2016) and serving as a judge for the Dezeen Awards.

Priya Khanchandani is a writer and curator whose work explores design as a lens to understand contemporary culture. She was previously Head of Curatorial and Interpretation at the Design Museum, where she led major exhibitions and research-driven projects. In 2023, she curated *The Offbeat Sari*, the first UK exhibition dedicated to the contemporary sari, examining its reinvention through material innovation and shifting cultural narratives. She was the first female editor of *Icon* magazine and has written widely on design, identity and visual culture, contributing to publications such as *The Observer*, *The Guardian*, *The Sunday Times*, *Financial Times*, *Frieze* and *Vogue*. She has also contributed to books and exhibition catalogues, including *Memphis: 40 Years of Kitsch and Elegance* (2021) and *Weird Sensation Feels Good: The World of ASMR* (2022).

Minnie Moll is Chief Executive of the Design Council, leading its Design for Planet mission that encourages designers of all stripes to tackle the climate crisis. Her career spans design, innovation, advertising and brand consultancy. She previously served as managing partner of HHCL and global marketing director at What If! As joint chief executive of the East of England Co-op, Moll was named ambassador for responsible business in the East of England in 2016 by King Charles III and was voted Vistage UK Business Leader of the Year in 2020. She has served on two Business Improvement District boards and a Town Deals Board. Moll is a passionate advocate for the power of design to drive social and environmental change, focusing on promoting regenerative design and addressing the climate crisis. Her leadership on Design for Planet was recognised with an Honorary Doctorate from the University of Westminster in 2024.

Jeremy Myerson is a design writer and researcher, and Professor Emeritus in the Helen Hamlyn Centre for Design at the Royal College of Art. He began his career as a journalist and was the founding editor of *Design Week* in 1986 before moving into academia, where he has focused on inclusive and socially engaged design. He co-founded the Helen Hamlyn Centre for Design and served as its director for sixteen years, leading research projects in ageing, health and work. Myerson is an Honorary Professorial Fellow at the University of Oxford's Institute of Population Ageing and Chairman of WORKTECH Academy, a global platform exploring the future of work which he co-founded in 2016. He has published more than twenty books on design's impact on society and business. His most recent books include *Designing a World for Everyone* (2021) and *Unworking: The Reinvention of the Modern Office* (2022).

Lynda Relph-Knight is a design writer and consultant who has played a key role in shaping discourse around design's impact on business, society and culture. She works with design organisations and consultancies to promote a greater understanding of design across disciplines and holds an honorary MA from the University for the Creative Arts, as well as honorary fellowships from Ravensbourne University and the Royal College of Art. She has served on advisory panels for the Associate Parliamentary Design & Innovation Group and the Sorrell Foundation's National Art & Design Saturday Club. As editor of Design Week for more than twenty years, she chronicled and critiqued developments in the design industry, covering everything from branding and product design to architecture and digital innovation. She continues to write about and within design, offering insights into its evolving role.

Ellie Runcie is Chief Design Officer at the BBC, where she leads user-experience design across all its digital products and services, ensuring they are easy to use, distinctive and deliver value for all audiences. Before joining the BBC in 2019, she led the Design Council's innovation strategy, shaping national programmes that embed design capabilities in key sectors, including manufacturing, health and education. She led Designing Demand – an £8m design support programme that enabled 5,000 businesses to adopt design capabilities and increase their performance. Over a ten-year period, these businesses grew by forty per cent, more than double that of a national control group. She also led the Design Council's public sector work, applying design approaches to address more than 100 societal challenges nationwide. Ellie played a key role in the development of the Design Council's Double Diamond in 2004 and, for the following twenty-two years, led its evolution and expansion across national and global design programmes, building a unique portfolio of methods and approaches that culminated in the Design Council's *Framework for Innovation*, published in 2019.

Sir John Sorrell CBE is a designer, philanthropist and champion of the UK's creative industries. He was Chair of the Design Council (1994–2000) and a UK Business Ambassador, appointed by successive prime ministers to promote Britain's creative excellence. He chaired CABE (2004–09) and UAL (2013–18) and conceived the London Design Festival, chairing it from 2003 to 2023. He co-founded the London Design Biennale, serving as its president (2016–23). With Lady Frances Sorrell CBE, he ran Newell & Sorrell (1976–2000) and founded the Sorrell Foundation in 1999 to inspire young people's creativity. They later established the National Saturday Club, a free creative programme for 13–16-year-olds. Sir John continues to be a key figure in advocating for design's role in education, business and culture.

Penny Sparke is Professor of Design History at Kingston University and Director of the Modern Interiors Research Centre. A leading scholar in design history for over four decades, she has published extensively on twentieth-century design, interiors and gender. She has taught at the University of Brighton and the Royal College of Art, and served as Dean of the Faculty of Art, Design and Music at Kingston University. Her books include *The Genius of Design* (2009), which accompanied a BBC Two documentary series, and *The Plastics Age* (1990), which complemented an exhibition at the V&A. Other key publications include *An Introduction to Design and Culture* (1986), *Design in Context* (1987), *As Long as It's Pink: The Sexual Politics of Taste* (1995) and *Nature Inside: Plants and Flowers in the Modern Interior* (2021). Her research has shaped critical discourse on domestic spaces, material culture, and the intersection of design and identity.

Deyan Sudjic is Distinguished Professor of Design and Architectural Studies at Lancaster University and Director Emeritus of the Design Museum, which he led from 2006 to 2020, overseeing its relocation to Kensington and its expansion as a global centre for design. He was an editor of *Domus* magazine in Milan; Director of the Venice Architecture Biennale; and has curated major exhibitions in Copenhagen, Istanbul and Tokyo, covering subjects from Zaha Hadid to Stanley Kubrick. His books include *The Language of Things* (2008), *B is for Bauhaus* (2014), *Stalin's Architect: Power and Survival in Moscow* (2022) and *John Pawson: Making Life Simpler* (2023). He was also the editor of *Design in Britain: Big Ideas (Small Island)* (2009).

Lesley Whitworth was, until recently, Deputy Curator and Senior Research Fellow at the University of Brighton Design Archives. Her involvement began with the founding deposit of the Design Council Archive in the mid-1990s, and as both teacher and curator, she has widened the audience for the Council's history while supporting scholarly engagement for many years. As a social and design historian, her work explores the role of material culture in shaping historical narratives, and her published research often focuses on the early history of the Council of Industrial Design (later the Design Council), particularly its advocacy for design and consumers. Her work has shed fresh light on the institutional frameworks that have influenced British design development.

Jonathan M. Woodham is Professor Emeritus of the History of Design and an associate of the Centre for Design History at the University of Brighton. A leading scholar in twentieth-century design history, he has published extensively since the 1970s, including *Twentieth Century Design* (1997) and *Dictionary of Modern Design* (2005; significantly enlarged and updated in 2016, with ongoing updates as part of Oxford Reference Online) – both key reference works. He has delivered keynote addresses in twenty-nine countries, acted as a peer reviewer for national and international research councils, and shaped design scholarship globally through board membership of leading journals and societies. He has played a significant role in advancing the academic study of design, particularly in relation to national identity, policy and industrial development. He is currently completing *British Design 1915–2025: Empire, Welfare State and Enterprise*, a monograph examining the evolving roles, economic and political complexities, and cultures of design in Britain.

Picture Credits

Every reasonable attempt has been made to identify owners of copyright. Errors and omissions notified to the publisher will be corrected in subsequent editions. Abbreviations are: A – above, B – below, C – centre, L – left, R – right.

pp.1, 2: Courtesy Design Council; pp.8, 9: Courtesy Liberty Archive; p.10: Photo Philip Sayer; p.11a: Image ID: DCA-30-1-7-6-1-2. Design Council Archive, University of Brighton Design Archives; p.11c: © the Design Museum; p.11b: The Design Council Slide Collection at Manchester Metropolitan University Special Collections; p.12: Photo Seth Taras. Courtesy Design Council; p.13l: Pentagram; p.13r: Courtesy Sir John Sorrell; p.17: New York Times Paris Bureau Collection; p.18: Image ID: 47-40. Design Council Archive, University of Brighton Design Archives; p.19: Image ID: DCA-30-7-3284. Design Council Archive, University of Brighton Design Archives; p.20: Victoria & Albert Museum, London; p.21a: Image ID: DCA-30-2-32-10. Design Council Archive, University of Brighton Design Archives; p.21b: Image ID: DCA-30-1-13-23-42 and 47-847. Design Council Archive, University of Brighton Design Archives; pp.22-3: Image ID: GB-1837-DES-DCA-30-2-30-1. Design Council Archive, University of Brighton Design Archives; p.24: Image ID: DCA-30-1-12-3-MA-83 and 48-3251. Design Council Archive, University of Brighton Design Archives; p.25a: Image ID: DCA-32-2-1-52-1. Design Council Archive, University of Brighton Design Archives; p.25b: Image ID: 47-1410. Design Council Archive, University of Brighton Design Archives; p.26a: Image ID: 48-40. Design Council Archive, University of Brighton Design Archives; p.26b: Design Council Archive, University of Brighton Design Archives; p.28: *Honeydew* design is © Liberty Fabric Limited 2025; p.31: The National Archives, London; p.32: Image ID: DCA-10-1-122. Design Council Archive, University of Brighton Design Archives; p.33: Image ID: 56-3387. Design Council Archive, University of Brighton Design Archives; p.34al: Image ID: DCA-30-2-1255. Design Council Archive, University of Brighton Design Archives; p.34ar: Design Council Archive, University of Brighton Design Archives; p.34bl: Design Council Archive, University of Brighton Design Archives; p.34br: Image ID: 59-1774. Design Council Archive, University of Brighton Design Archives; p.35a: Image ID: DCA-10-1-81. Design Council Archive, University of Brighton Design Archives; p.35b: Design Council Archive, University of Brighton Design Archives; p.36a: Image ID: 583285 8810. Design Council Archive, University of Brighton Design Archives; p.36b: The Design Council Slide Collection at Manchester Metropolitan University Special Collections; p.37: Image ID: 1528 - 6590. Design Council Archive, University of Brighton Design Archives; p.39a: Photo Designmuseum Danmark; p.39b: *Woman* magazine, March 1950; p.40: Image ID: DCA-30-2-628.199. Design Council Archive, University of Brighton Design Archives; p.41l: Image ID: DCA-30-2-4932. Design Council Archive, University of Brighton Design Archives; p.41r: The Design Council Slide Collection at Manchester Metropolitan University Special Collections; pp.42-3: TfL from the London Transport Museum collection; p.44l: Ercol; p.44r: Victoria and Albert Museum, London; p.45: © Robin & Lucienne Day Foundation; p.46, 47: The Design Council Slide Collection at Manchester Metropolitan University Special Collections; p.48: *Meteor* design is © Liberty Fabric Limited 2025; p.51: Jaguar Daimler Heritage Trust/Alamy Stock Photo; p.52: Image ID: DCA-10-1-99. Design Council Archive, University of Brighton Design Archives; p.53: Image ID: DCA-10-1-65. Design Council Archive, University of Brighton Design Archives; p.54a: Image ID: DCA-10-1-124. Design Council Archive, University of Brighton Design Archives; p.54bl: Design Council Archive, University of Brighton Design Archives; p.54br: Image ID: A7768-25. Design Council Archive, University of Brighton Design Archives; p.55a: Image ID: DCA-10-1-153. Design Council Archive, University of Brighton Design Archives; p.55c: Image ID: DCA-30-7-1969-12-1. Design Council Archive, University of Brighton Design Archives; p.55b: Image ID: DCA-10-1-145. Design Council Archive, University of Brighton Design Archives; p.56a: Image ID: 65-1346. Design Council Archive, University of Brighton Design Archives; p.56b: Image ID: DCA-10-1-125. Design Council Archive, University of Brighton Design Archives; p.57: Image ID: DCA-30-7-1963-9-1. Design Council Archive, University of Brighton Design Archives; p.59: © Apple Corps Ltd.; p.60: HABANS Patrice/Paris Match via Getty Images; p.61: Ben Martin/Getty Images; p.62a: Courtesy Christopher Breward; pp.62b, 63: The Design Council Slide Collection at Manchester Metropolitan University Special Collections; p.64l: Design Council Archive, University of Brighton Design Archives; p.64r: AMHCA (Association of Members of Hornsey College of Art). Courtesy David Page; p.66: © Crown Copyright, The National Archives, London; p.67: The Design Council Slide Collection at Manchester Metropolitan University Special Collections; p.68a: Rosetti design is © Liberty Fabric Limited 2025; p.68b: *Frieze* design is © Liberty Fabric Limited 2025; p.71: Image Jamie Reid. Copyright Sex Pistols Residuals; p.72: Image ID: DCA-10-1-9. Design Council Archive, University of Brighton Design Archives; p.73a: Image ID: DCA-30-1-7-6-3-1. Design Council Archive, University of Brighton Design Archives; p.73c: Image ID: DCA-10-1-30. Design Council Archive, University of Brighton Design Archives; p.73b: Image ID: DCA-30-1-7-6-2-1. Design Council Archive, University of Brighton Design Archives; pp.74-5: Image ID: DCA-30-7-1978-24-1. Design Council Archive, University of Brighton Design Archives; p.76al: Image ID: DCA-10-1-183. Design Council Archive, University of Brighton Design Archives; p.76ar: Image ID: DCA-10-1-17. Design Council Archive, University of Brighton Design Archives; p.76b: Image ID: DCA-30-7-1972-2-1. Design Council Archive, University of Brighton Design Archives; p.79: Keystone Press/Alamy Stock Photo; p.80l: Wolff Olins; p.80r: Windsor and Newton Artists Inks.; p.81l: © the Design Museum; p.81r: The Metropolitan Museum of Art/Art Resource/Scala, Florence; p.82: The Design Council Slide Collection at Manchester Metropolitan University Special Collections; p.84: Image ID: DCA-30-7-1972-17-1. Design Council Archive, University of Brighton Design Archives; p.85: Courtesy Vivienne Westwood archive; p.86: Photo Duffy © Duffy Archive; p.87a: Special Collections. Royal College of Art; p.87b: Crafts Council Collection: W21. Photo Todd-White Art Photography; p.88: *Trellis Paisley* design is © Liberty Fabric Limited 2025; p.91: Mike Kemp/In Pictures via Getty Images; p.93: Image ID: DCA-10-1-134. Design Council Archive, University of Brighton Design Archives; p.94a: Image ID: DCA-30-7-1986-6-1. Design Council Archive, University of Brighton Design Archives; p.94bl: Image ID: c9344-7. Design Council Archive, University of Brighton Design Archives; p.94br: Image ID: DCA-10-1-138. Design Council Archive, University of Brighton Design Archives; p.95al: Image ID: DCA-30-7-1989-12-1. Design Council Archive, University of Brighton Design Archives; p.95ar: Image ID: DCA-30-7-1985-11-1. Design Council Archive, University of Brighton Design Archives; p.95b: Image ID: DCA-30-7-1988-19-1. Design Council Archive, University of Brighton Design Archives; p.96: Image ID: DCA-10-1-205. Design Council Archive, University of Brighton Design Archives; p.97: Image ID: DCA-10-1-161. Design Council Archive, University of Brighton Design Archives; p.99: Archimage/Alamy Stock Photo; p.100a: © British Airways; p.100b: BT Group; p.101: Courtesy Anna Arca; pp.102-3: © Ben Kelly & Morph; p.104: © the Design Museum; p.105l: Laurie Sagalyn/WWD/Penske Media via Getty Images; p.105r: Photo Vinmag Archive; p.106: © the Design Museum; p.107a: Photo Ian Dobbie; p.107b: Photo Peter Cook; p.108: *Memphis Leaf* design is © Liberty Fabric Limited 2025; p.111: Guy Marineau/Conde Nast via Getty Images; p.113: Courtesy Sir John Sorrell; pp.114, 115: Courtesy Design Council; p.117: European Union (EU)/Council of Europe (CoE); p.118l: © International Olympic Committee (IOC); p.118r: © Orange 2025; p.119: Courtesy Daljit Singh; pp.120-1: Troika/Alamy Stock Photo; p.122a: © 2025 Heathrow Express; pp.122bl, 122br: ©2025 STARCK; p.123: Tom Dixon Studio; p.124-5: Russell Kord ARCHIVE/Alamy Stock Photo; p.126: Courtesy Herman Miller, Inc.; p.127: Deepend. London Designer Fred Flade; p.128: Vanessa design is © Liberty Fabric Limited 2025; p.131: © Krivinis/Dreamstime.com; p.133: Photo Seth Taras. Courtesy Design Council; p.134, 135, 136: Courtesy Design Council; p.137: Pearson Lloyd Design Ltd; p.139: Tom Dixon Studio; p.140a: Photo (c) Katsuhisa Kida. Courtesy RSHP; p.140c: Courtesy London Design Festival; p.140b: Jasper Morrison Ltd; p.141: Fairchild Archive/Penske Media via Getty Images; pp.142-3: Werner Huthmacher; p.144bl: Apple Inc.; p.144br: Tŷ Nant, Spring Water Ltd.; p.145: © Micha Weidmann Studio; p.146a: Studio Waldemeyer; p.146b: Alessandro Paderni for Moroso; p.147: © Nigel Young/Foster and Partners; p.148: *Small Susanna* design is © Liberty Fabric Limited 2025; p.151: Led By Donkeys Ltd; pp.153, 154a: Courtesy Design Council; p.154b: Government Digital Service. © Crown copyright; p.155: Government Design Principles. © Crown copyright; p.156a: Courtesy Stella McCartney; p.156c: (c) LOCOG; p.156b: Ian MacNicol/Getty Images; p.157: Hufton+Crow/View Pictures/Universal Images Group via Getty Images; p.159: The Occupied Times; p.160a: Greenpeace; p.160b: North Design; p.161l: © Fuzja44/Dreamstime.com; p.161r: © 2025 ustwo games; pp.162-3: Courtesy London Design Festival; p.164l: Courtesy Christopher Raeburn; p.164r: Courtesy JW Anderson; p.165l: Photo Daniel L. Lu; p.165r: Photo G. GARDNER; p.166a: Led By Donkeys Ltd; p.166b: Photo Tzortzis Rallis; p.167a: Wirestock/Dreamstime.com; p.167b: Justice4Grenfell Campaign Ltd/Jeff Moore; p.168: *Tresco* design is © Liberty Fabric Limited 2025; p.171: © Crossrail Ltd; p.173: Courtesy Design Council; p.174a: SPIN Studio; p.174c: Elizabeth Lock - Rawframed/rawframed.com; p.174b: Courtesy Design Council; p.175: Photo Alan Richardson. Courtesy Design Council; p.176a: Courtesy Design Council; p.176b: Photo Sonny Malhotra. Courtesy Design Council; p.177: Courtesy Design Council; p.179: © Ladyligeia/Dreamstime.com; p.180a: James Tye Photography; p.180c: © William Barton/Dreamstime.com; p.180b: Photo Justin Haigh; p.181: © John Gomez/Dreamstime.com; p.182l: Courtesy Design Council; p.182r: © Archivio Storico della Biennale di Venezia-ASAC/Photo Matteo De Mayda; p.183: Photo Iwan Baan. © Counterspace; pp.184-5: Photo Toby Coulson; p.186a: Photo Paul Plews. Courtesy James Shaw; p.186b: © Andy Stagg; p.187: © Felix Speller for the Design Museum; p.188a: *Lines Ballet* design is © Liberty Fabric Limited 2025; p.188b: *Soho* design is © Liberty Fabric Limited 2025; p.191a: *Linear Leaf* design is © Liberty Fabric Limited 2025; p.191b: *Autumn Grove* design is © Liberty Fabric Limited 2025.

Networks, Conversations and Collaborations: The Design Council Archive

In 1994, Brighton academics Professor Jonathan M. Woodham and Dr Paddy Maguire made a bold strategic move, proposing the University of Brighton's Department of Design History as the new home for the Design Council's archive. As one of the institutions where Design History emerged as a discipline, Brighton was a fitting choice. The archive became a vital resource for new research into the Council and British design, shaped by its first curatorial staff Dr Catherine Moriarty and Dr Lesley Whitworth. Over time it has been joined by more than twenty other collections, including the archives of designers involved in the Council's work as well as international design organisations WDO (formerly ICSID) and IcoD (formerly Icograda). These additions have enriched the University of Brighton Design Archives, but the Design Council remains its largest and most significant collection. It documents the Design Council's bold ambition, as declared in its first annual report, to improve design in British industry through government sponsorship. Today, it continues to attract researchers from around the world as well as Brighton's own students and scholars.

At the heart of the archive are hundreds of meticulously maintained files, following the Civil Service 'Registry' system, which record the Council's early activities. These documents capture the ideas, exchanges, decisions, disagreements and ambitions that shaped its work. Alongside these, the archive contains a remarkable photographic collection, not only documenting the Council's exhibitions and events but also featuring reference images of products and environments. Other key materials include a striking series of posters and an extensive library of the Council's publishing activities, notably its renowned journal *Design*.

Together, these records provide more than a history of a government-sponsored design organisation. They reveal the networks, conversations and collaborations that have shaped British design – offering a lens through which to view the objects, environments and aesthetics of daily life.

Text by Sue Breakell, Archive Director and Principal Research Fellow for the University of Brighton Design Archives

Acknowledgements

The Design Council wishes to thank the many contributors who made this project possible.

To the University of Brighton Design Archives for their time, expertise and invaluable stewardship of the Design Council's historical records, and to the Design Council Slide Collection at Manchester Metropolitan University for sharing their collection from 1945–90.

To our creative partners, Liberty, who are celebrating their own landmark anniversary in their 150th year. Their exquisite archival prints bring each decade to life, and our collaboration on the new Liberty x Design Council print for 2025 will be a cherished part of the World Design Congress London celebrations. Special mention to Andrea Petochi, Mary-Ann Dunkley, Silvia Spagnol and Emma Fowler.

To Park Communications for sharing our vision of planet-friendly book production. Their expertise in environmentally responsible materials has ensured this book is produced to the highest sustainability standards. Our thanks also to Sappi, whose responsibly sourced paper made this publication possible. Special mention to Peter Appleton for his support throughout this project.

To our funding partners at Arts and Humanities Research Council (AHRC) for their continuous support in championing British design.

To our friends at Pentagram, for generously hosting us at their studio to launch this project.

The Design Council's eighty-year history would not have been possible without the dedication of those who have worked there over the years. We thank colleagues past and present, including those at the time of publication:

Ishbel Allotey, Maariyah Amejee, Mark Anonuevo, Maryam Atta, Rachel Bronstein, Matthew Burgess, Rebecca Busch, Laura Casali, Hilary Cuddy, Fiona Dahl, Kim Davids, Cat Drew, Irene Hakansson, Ed Hobson, Rob Holmes, Rachel Hutchison, Jessie Johnson, Alex McCorkindale, Minnie Moll, Rachel Moriarty, Flora Newbigin, Feyidara Olawuyi, Harriet Packer, Polly Raymond, Bronwen Rees, Anna Roberts, Josephine Ryan Gill, Susana Soares, Sarah Stallwood-Hall, Helen Topham, Nikki van Grimbergen, Owen Wainhouse and Fred Weissenborn.

We also acknowledge those who have served on the Board of Trustees over the years, including our current Chair, William Eccleshare, Deputy Chair, Jonquil Hackenberg and Trustees Anne Boddington, Beatrice Fraenkel, Biljana Savic, Chris Naylor, Keith Morgan, Paul Monaghan and Tendai Chetse.

Design Council

designcouncil.org.uk

First published in 2025
© 2025 Design Council

ISBN 978-1-3999-9790-4

All rights reserved. No part of this publication may be reproduced, stored in a retrieval system or transmitted, in any form by any means, electronic, mechanical, photocopying, recording or otherwise, without the prior permission of Design Council.

Editor: Mark Cortes Favis
Project Editor: Laura Casali
Editorial Advisor: Kim Davids
Picture Researcher: Anabel Navarro
Copyeditor: Simon Coppock
Proofreader: Ian McDonald
Design: Chris Benfield

Many colleagues at the Design Council have supported this book, and thanks go to them all.

Distribution
Thames & Hudson
181A High Holborn
London WC1V 7QX
United Kingdom
thamesandhudson.com

This book has been manufactured within ISO 14001 environmental standards, using FSC papers and vegetable-based inks, by Park Communications Ltd, London. Park is a member of Graphius Group.